The People & Places of CONSTANTINOPLE

WATERCOLOURS BY AMADEO COUNT PREZIOSI 1816–1882

♦

Briony Llewellyn and Charles Newton

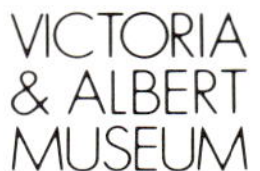

With assistance from J Sainsbury plc

ISBN 0 948107 03 0

Published by The Victoria and Albert Museum 1985

Designed by Grant Morrison
Printed by Precision Press London

Front cover: Detail of Ladies in an Araba c.1843-50

Preface

This is the first exhibition of the work of Amadeo Preziosi to be held in this country. It does not claim to be definitive, but is centered on the Museum's substantial holdings and augmented by loans from collections in Great Britain. Preziosi's name is now little known except to specialists, but in the period 1840-70 he was by far the most renowned artist in Constantinople. He was only retrieved from the critical neglect into which he had fallen in the 20th century by Rodney Searight who began to appreciate his importance while building up his unsurpassed collection of views of the Near and Middle East. Indeed, it is fitting that the exhibition honours not only Preziosi himself but also Rodney Searight, pioneer of the study of this field, whose collection the Museum is raising funds to acquire. It is hoped that the enthusiasm Preziosi's contemporaries felt for his lively and colourful studies of a now vanished way of life will be appreciated by visitors to the exhibition.

The exhibition has been organised by Briony Llewellyn and Charles Newton and they would like to thank the following people for their help and advice:– Nagla Atiye, Duncan Bull, Sally Chappell, Rosemary Crill, Chevalier Joseph Galea, Alexander Gimson, Godfrey Goodwin, Helen Guiterman, Mary Beal, Niall Hobhouse, Liselotte Jensen, Jacques Mantoura, Pippa Mason, Lady Millar, Dorothy Newton, Neşe Öymen, Baroncino Nicholas da Piro, Contino Dr. Josef Preziosi, Gill Saunders, Rodney Searight, Theresa Searight, Janet Skidmore, Jane Stevens, Mary Anne Stevens, Tania Szrejber, Lynne Thornton.

C M Kauffmann
Keeper of Prints and Drawings and Paintings

Introduction

'There is, perhaps, no country under heaven where it is more difficult for an European to obtain a full and perfect insight into the national character, than in Turkey.'[1]

Miss Julia Pardoe, who made this observation in her detailed and perceptive account of Constantinople, *The City of the Sultan*, published in 1837, was one of the western Europeans in the 19th century who did reach some understanding of the Turkish way of life. Another, who used images instead of words to express his own appreciation of the complexity and diversity of the Turkish character, was the artist, Amadeo Preziosi. In addition to this rare insight, Presiozi possessed considerable abilities as a draughtsman. In recent years neither of these qualities have received the attention they deserve. During his lifetime Preziosi's talents were held in high regard, the popular weekly, *Illustrated London News*, describing him in 1859 as 'the well-known artist of Oriental subjects' and Murray's *Handbook for Travellers in Turkey* of 1871 recommending his 'coloured sketches'.[2] In the early years of this century the author of a book on Turkish artists referred to him as 'l'aquarelliste levantin' who in 1874 had been almost the sole representative of *Turkish* art.[3] Nowadays, if Preziosi's art is recognised at all, it is in Turkey and Malta rather than in France or England, and even there, knowledge is not widespread.[4] The renown which he achieved in his own time has been all but forgotten.

This exhibition presents an opportunity for his work to be reassessed. Its core is a substantial holding of watercolours purchased by the Victoria and Albert Museum early in this century. These consist mainly of two separate groups, one of the Constantinople characters frequently depicted by Preziosi (cat. nos. 1-14), the other, more distinctive, of portraits (cat. nos. 15-36). The Museum's holdings are supplemented by loans, in particular from the Searight Collection (cat. nos. 42, 43, 45-48, 50, 51, 53).

By birth a member of the wealthy, aristocratic, strongly Catholic families of Malta, Amadeo, 5th Count Preziosi espoused the very different environment of cosmopolitan Constantinople, at that time still the capital of the vast and heterogenous, but predominantly Islamic, Ottoman Empire. A resident of the city for nearly half a century, Preziosi became familiar with almost every aspect of its life, from the entourages of the foreign diplomats and other Christian inhabitants of Pera and Galata to the mainly Muslim population of Stamboul on the other side of the Golden Horn. Few Franks[5] acquired more than a superficial knowledge of the old city and fewer still were acquainted with its people and their traditions. Preziosi came to know them well enough to represent them in paint with remarkable accuracy and understanding, but at the same time he remained part of the Christian community. For four decades from the 1840s to the 1870s he supplied images of Constantinople life and scenery to countless travellers from the West for them to take home as souvenirs of their visit, much like picture post-cards today. He was so well established that his own studio 'full of knick-knacks and sketches' itself became one of Constantinople's tourist attractions, and was visited by several eminent travellers.[6]

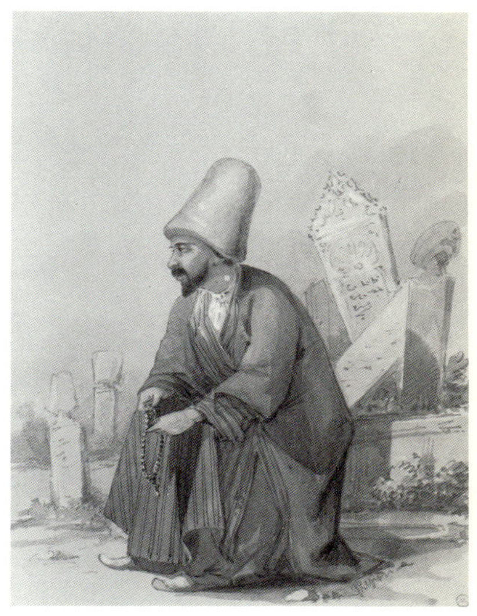

7 A Mevlevî in a Cemetry c. 1843

Amadeo Preziosi was born in Malta on 2 December 1816, and baptised in the parish church of Porto Salvo in Valletta with the names of Aloysius, Rosarius, Amadeus, Raymondus and Andreas. His family, originally pirates who settled in the island at the end of the seventeenth century, was ennobled by King Amadeo of Sicily in 1718, and had held important posts in Malta's administration during the eighteenth century. His father, Giovanni Francesco, had been a representative of the Maltese nobility during negotiations for the Treaty of Amiens in 1802 when the island came under British rule. Intending that his eldest son should play a significant part in the island's new administrative system devised by the Governor, Sir Thomas Maitland, he sent him to study law. The young Preziosi, however, was already more interested in art and began his study of it in the studio of Giuseppe Hyzler, an artist higly regarded in Malta and a follower of the Nazarene School founded in Rome by Friedrich Overbeck. Sometime in his early twenties, c.1840, Preziosi went to Paris with his brother Leandro. While Leandro studied the newly discovered photographic processes, Amadeo continued to develop his artistic talents with one of the teachers at the École des Beaux Arts. Little is known of his life in Paris, nor with whom he associated, but he would no doubt have absorbed some of the prevailing artistic taste and styles. He would certainly have known the lithographs of Honoré Daumier who by 1840 had been forced to replace his political satires of the 1830s with the more humorous, rapidly-sketched scenes of everyday life which may have made a significant impression on Preziosi. Another source for Preziosi's interest in contemporary figures in real rather than imaginary environments, may well have been *Les Français peints par eux-mêmes*, a large publication comprising illustrated essays on French types by a variety of artists and authors. The first volume appeared in 1839, and was extremely popular, continuing until 1876.

On his return to Malta, Preziosi found his father no less antagonistic to his artistic inclinations than before, and only by leaving the island could he hope to pursue his own choice of career.

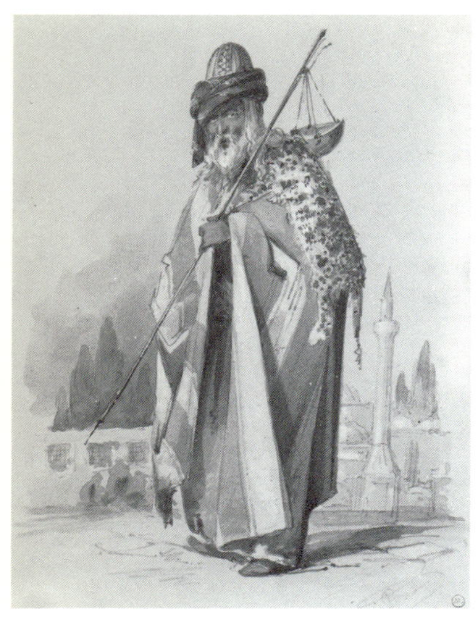

8 A Dervish with a Leopard-Skin c. 1843

The place he selected for his escape was Constantinople, for reasons which, in the absence of any declared motives, must be surmised. Malta, in the middle of the Mediterranean, was visited by many travellers en route between western Europe and the Near East. Several of its indigenous artists found their way eastwards, and in particular to Constantinople. Among these were several members of the Schranz family who made their living by drawing views in Turkey, Egypt, Syria and Palestine, as well as Malta, for gentleman travellers. One of Giovanni Schranz's (1794-1882) specialities seems to have been large panoramic views of Constantinople, often on several sheets of paper joined together, with buildings and shipping delinated in minute detail. Some of these can be dated c. 1832-34, but he certainly visited the city more than once. Another Maltese artist active in Constantinople around this time was Luigi Brocktorff.[7] If, as is likely, Preziosi knew something of the work of these artists, this may well have contributed to his decision to see Constantinople for himself.

An additional incentive must have been Constantinople's renown as an exotic eastern metropolis. Its attractions were appositely expressed by Julia Pardoe in her preface to *The Beauties of the Bosphorus* (1837-39), a popular series of engravings after William Bartlett (1809-54) for which she supplied the descriptive texts. 'Constantinople needs no aid from the imagination to make it one of the brightest gems in the diadem of nature: its clear calm sky, its glittering sea, its amphitheatre of thickly-peopled hills, its geographical position, its political importance, and, above all, its surpassing novelty, tend to make every day and every hour in that gorgeous scene, and under that sunny sky, a season of intense enjoyment; while the varying character of the native population, constituted as it is of such anomalous material – the truthful Turk, the wily Greek, the stately Armenian, and the timid Jew – coupled with the blended air of mystery and of magnificence which pervades the whole locality, suffice to render the Turkish metropolis a sojourn of unwearied and exciting delight.'[8]

Most western visitors were spell-bound by their first view of the city. The effusions quoted in Murray's *Turkey* are typical: 'At last, Constantinople rose in all its grandeur before us. With eyes riveted on the expanding splendours, I watched, as they rose out of the bosom of the surrounding waters, the pointed minarets – the swelling cupolas – and the innumerable habitations, either stretching along the jagged shore, or reflecting their image in the mirror of the deep, or creeping up the crested mountain, and tracing their outline in the expanse of the sky'. So entranced was this visitor that he hardly dared breathe for fear that he 'might dispel the glorious vision and find its whole fabric only a delusive dream'.[9] Such raptures were not for Alexander Kinglake, who in *Eothen* related his own tour of the Levant in 1834-35 with brevity and wit. While scoffing at such purple passages he too expressed his delight in the city: 'Even if we don't take part in the chant about "mosques and minarets" we can still yield praises to Stamboul'.[10] Ignoring the advice of fellow Franks, Kinglake wandered happily through the old city's plague-ridden streets.

With travel facilitated by the expansion of both railways and steam navigation, more western European tourists were coming to Constantinople, but few were as intrepid as Kinglake or Miss Pardoe. During the two years she spent in Constantinople in the company of her father, Miss Pardoe gained access to Turkish society, both high and low, and discovered many of the prejudices of her own culture to be fallacious. Most Franks were content to admire the skyline of Stamboul from the comparatively safe and familiar confines of Pera. They, as much as their compatriots who remained at home, fostered the myths and inaccuracies which clouded western ideas of the East. As Julia Pardoe commented with her usual acumen: 'The European mind has become so imbued with ideas of Oriental mysteriousness, mysticism, and magnificence, and it has been so long accustomed to pillow its faith on the marvels and metaphors of tourists, that it is to be doubted whether it will willingly cast off its old associations and suffer itself to be undeceived'.[11] William Bartlett's eighty illustrations to Pardoe's *Beauties of the Bosphorus* aimed to reveal the splendours of Constantinople to westerners. Similar and equally successful was *Constantinople and the Scenery of the Seven Churches of Asia Minor* published by Fisher (1839), with text by the Rev. Robert Walsh, formerly chaplain to the British Embassy in Constantinople, and illustrations by, among others, Thomas Allom (1804-72). Here were topographically accurate views of the city's famous scenes – its mosques and bazaars, its cemeteries and *hamams*, the Seraglio, the Golden Horn, the Sweet Waters of Europe and of Asia, to name but a few – rendered by artists who had seen and sketched them for themselves during the 1830s. For the tourist who had visited these places and for the countless more armchair travellers who had not, they were authentic enough. They met the western European demand for realistic pictorial representations of exotic people and places but did not disturb their preconceived romantic notions of them. They show Constantinople through rose-tinted spectacles, warm and alluring, exotic but not alien, sometimes dilapidated but never squalid, and always thoroughly picturesque. Bartlett and Allom are the best known of the artists in the first half of the nineteenth century through whose eyes the life and scenery of Constantinople was exposed to the West. Through the medium of engraving and lithography, their images reached a wide market; even today they are to be seen in reproduction all over Istanbul. By the time Preziosi came to the city, then, the supply of such images was already a well established occupation for artists.

It is not certain when Preziosi arrived in Constantinople, but it seems to have been by November 1842, the date on a group of drawings of Constantinople subjects.[12] At about this time he may also have met Robert Curzon who was the British Ambassador,

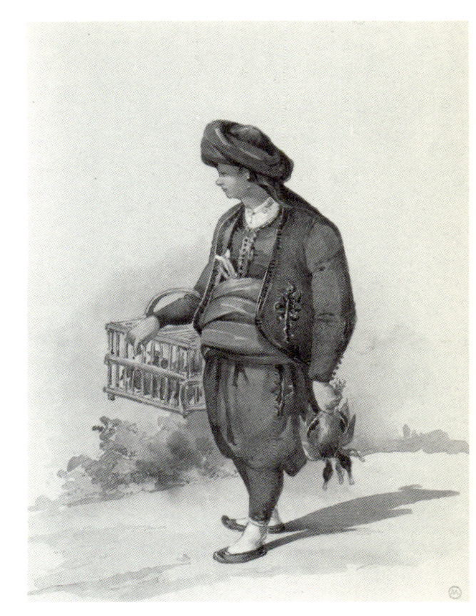

11 A Duck-Seller c. 1843

Lord Stratford de Redcliffe's private secretary, before he left on a special mission to Erzerum in January 1843. Either then or when passing through Constantinople on his way home a year later, Curzon, who 'greatly preferred a ramble in the bazaars or among the ruined vestiges of Old Stamboul to the copying of even the most exciting of his chief's famous despatches',[13] commissioned a series of drawings of typical Constantinople characters from Preziosi.[14] So too, apparently, did another, unidentified Frank (probably British), since there is another very similar series of characters, three of which are dated 1843, now in the Victoria and Albert Museum (cat. nos. 1-14)[15]. That year Preziosi also drew a porttrait of Sir Henry Layard in Bakhtiyari dress, dated 6 April 1843, which was later reproduced in lithograph as the frontispiece to the famous archaeologist's *Early Adventures in Persia, Susiana and Babylonia*

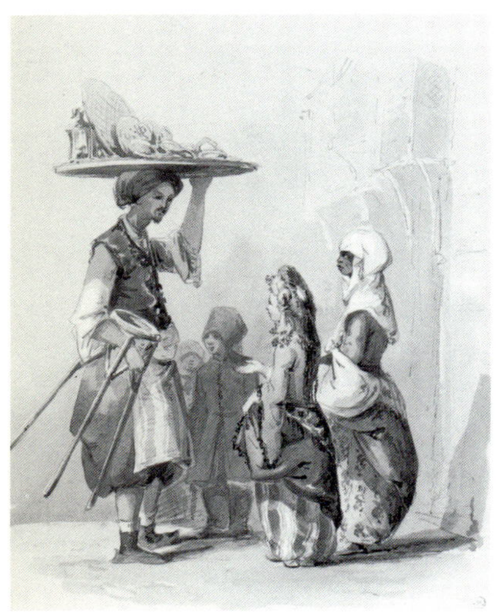

13 A Simit-Seller or Simitçi c. 1843

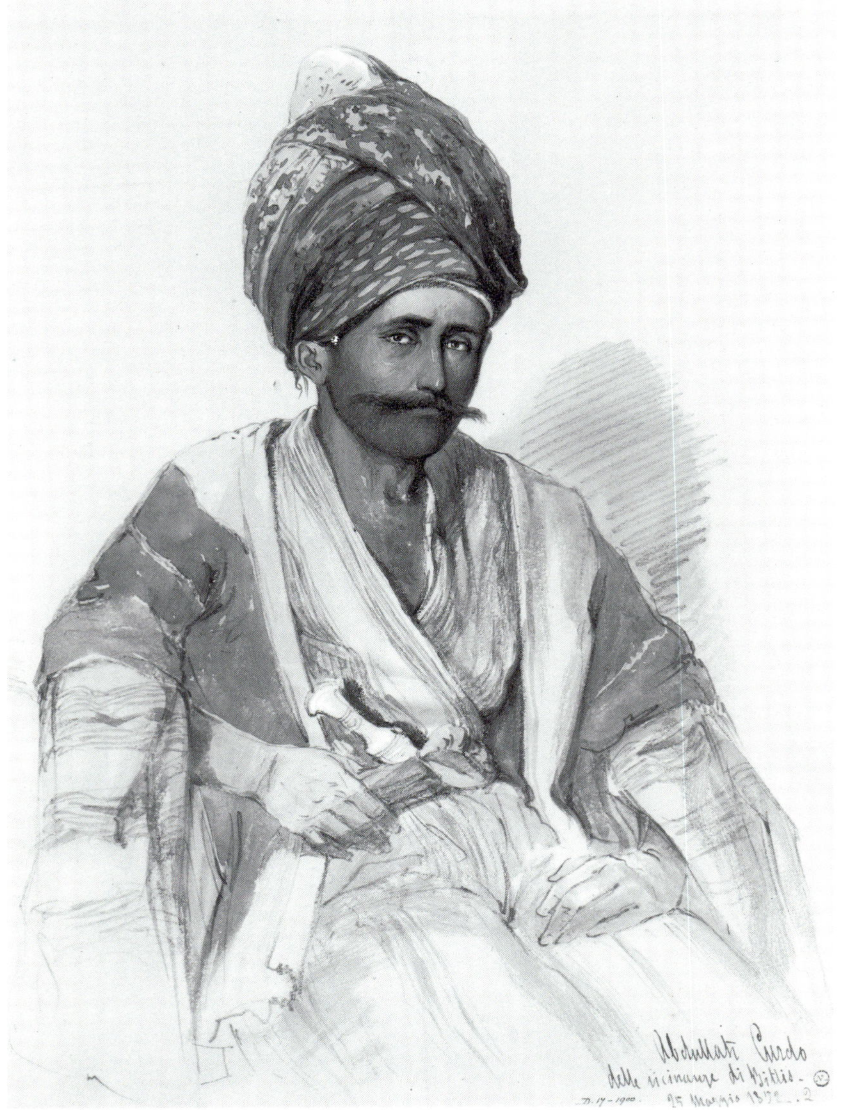

16 Abdullah, a Kurd from the region of Bitlis 1852

(1887).[16] From all these commissions it is evident that in the early 1840s Preziosi rapidly established a reputation as a painter of the contemporary life of Constantinople. Living in Pera, in Hamalbaşı Sokağı, with a Greek wife by whom he had three daughters and a son,[17] he became a well-known figure in the Frankish community, especially in British diplomatic circles. At the same time he familiarised himself with Turkish manners and customs. His native tongue was Italian; he undoubtedly spoke French, and probably also some Greek and English, and may also have acquired some Turkish. That he was, reputedly, at some time Assistant Political Dragoman at the British Embassy, and subsequently First Dragoman of the Greek Legation, is a further indication of his ability to cross cultural boundaries.[18]

Preziosi's staple subjects were the ordinary inhabitants of Constantinople. Both the Curzon and the Victoria and Albert Museum albums bring many of these together, revealing the extraordinary cultural diversity of the city's large population. In addition to Turks of varying descriptions – merchants, street vendors, soldiers, dervishes, and women – there are, among other nationalities, Greeks, Albanians, Circassians, Armenians, Bulgarians, Jews, Kurds and Nubians – all representatives of the different components of the still extensive Ottoman Empire.

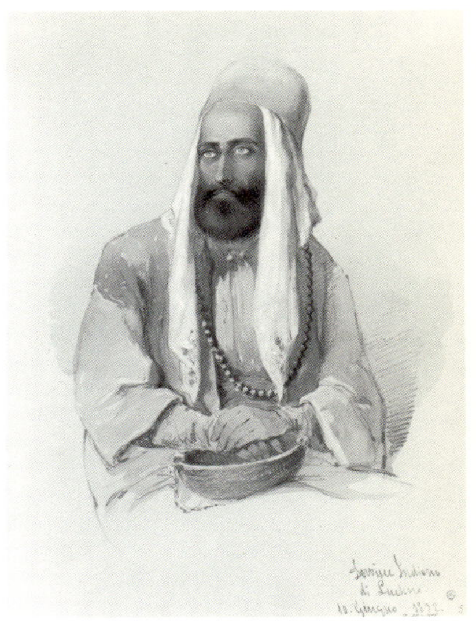

18 An Indian Dervish from Lucknow 1852

Several artists before Preziosi had depicted Constantinople characters, but usually high-ranking members of the establishment and primarily for the sake of their exotic and colourful costume. A notable series of this kind is that by William Page (1794-1872) c.1810-20, which include a *Janissary*, an *Armenian Lady* and a *Persian Prince*.[19] Page's figures are seen in isolation with no indication of their environment. Preziosi's by contrast are set in the context of their everyday existence: the barber is at work in his shop, towel and basin to hand (cat. no. 10), the Bulgarian shepherd minds his flock (cat. no. 12), the odalisque reclines on the soft cushions of her harem apartment (cat. no. 43), the dervish counts his beads and meditates in a cemetery (cat. no. 7). It is as if the spectator has turned a corner and interrupted them in the course of their daily lives.

For at least the first decade of his career in Constantinople, Preziosi's drawings of these 'types' were in great demand among tourists, who commissioned or purchased them as mementoes of their visit. The Victoria and Albert Museum's examples, probably all datable to c.1843, are of high quality and may have been the prototypes on which subsequent similar series were based. There are versions of some of them in the Curzon album of 1844, somewhat inferior in both colouring and draughtsmanship. Other isolated examples of this genre such as the *Women at a Street Fountain* (cat. no. 42) may once have been part of a series. Two versions of the *Harem Scene* showing an odalisque with her cup of coffee and smoking her *çubuk*, attended by her Nubian slave-girl, are known to exist, one of 1851, the other, coarser in detail, of 1852 (see cat. no. 43). Preziosi made copies of these popular subjects to

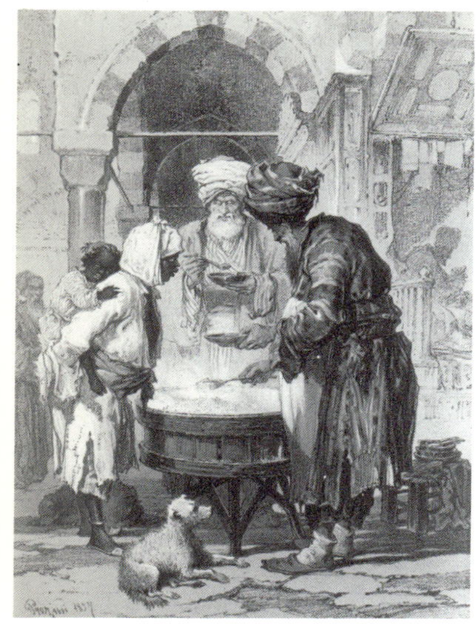

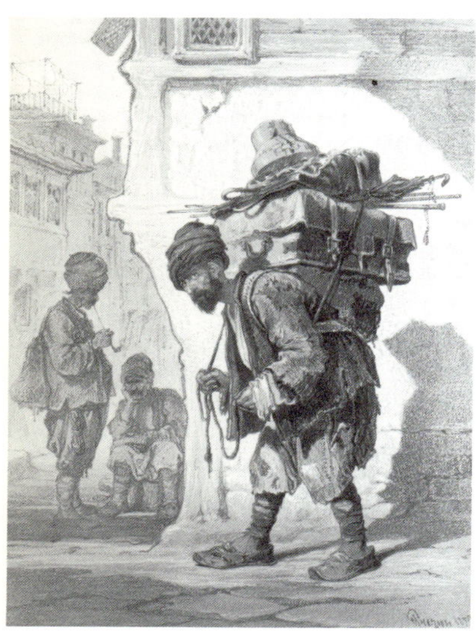

Top: Pilau

Bottom: Hamal

Opposite: Coffee House

Illustrations from *Stamboul. Recollections of Eastern Life*.

order, and may well have employed studio assistants to meet the increasing demand.

The popularity of Preziosi's Constantinople 'types' prompted him, some years later, to embark on a series of lithographs. These were published in 1858 by Lemercier, the foremost lithographic house in Paris in the mid 19th century, and there is little doubt that Preziosi travelled to Paris to oversee the project. By then colour lithography was well established, but printers and artists were constantly experimenting with new techniques. According to family tradition, Preziosi pioneered a process which more faithfully reproduced both the gradation and density of tone of the original drawings. No lithographer's name appears on the prints, an unusual omission suggesting that the artist himself did the drawing on the stones and used the process he had developed for the printing. In the 1883 reprint of the album, the prints are lettered, *Preziosi del et lith.*

The album, entitled *Stamboul. Recollections of Eastern Life*, consists of 29 plates, and a frontispiece. Each plate encapsulates a slice of Constantinople life: women fingering the quality of silk materials in the bazaar; an old man serving *pilau* to a negro woman with her child; prosperous, well-dressed Greeks emerging from church, while beggars wait at the door; women picnicing at the Sweet Waters of Asia; a *hamal* bent under the weight of a tourist's luggage, complete with umbrella, walking stick and top hat; a widow and her child in a cemetery; dervishes whirling in their *tekke*. The figures, their costume, accessories and settings are authentic in every detail, but the overall impression is mannered. Preziosi has telescoped reality in order to impart as much information as possible about his subject. In the *Coffee House*, for example, are all the characters one might expect to find in a Turkish café – the old man smoking his pipe, the handsome Greek, the youthful waiter and the laughing musician – but, crammed together to fill almost every inch of the picture space, they appear larger than life. Poses and facial expressions are exaggerated, sometimes to the point of caricature, to convey more clearly the essential nature of the scene: the Michelangelesque *contraposto* of the Greek boatman emphasises his brawny physique; in the *Water Carrier* an old man leers at a young girl who coyly half draws her veil across her face (see cat. no. 52). Compositional devices such as foreshortening perspective, highlighting two or three figures in strong colour against a near monochrome background, and turning one of the figures to look out of the picture, are also employed to heighten the drama of the interchanges between the characters and involve the spectator more directly in the action.

In all this Preziosi's lithographs are very different from his much more naturalistic watercolours of the people and places of Constantinople. In *A Turkish Coffee-House* (cat. no. 46) for example, the same types appear but are a more integral part of the whole scene. This is not a simplified, tourist's image of a café, but the place as a Turk would have seen it, and with a far more subtle

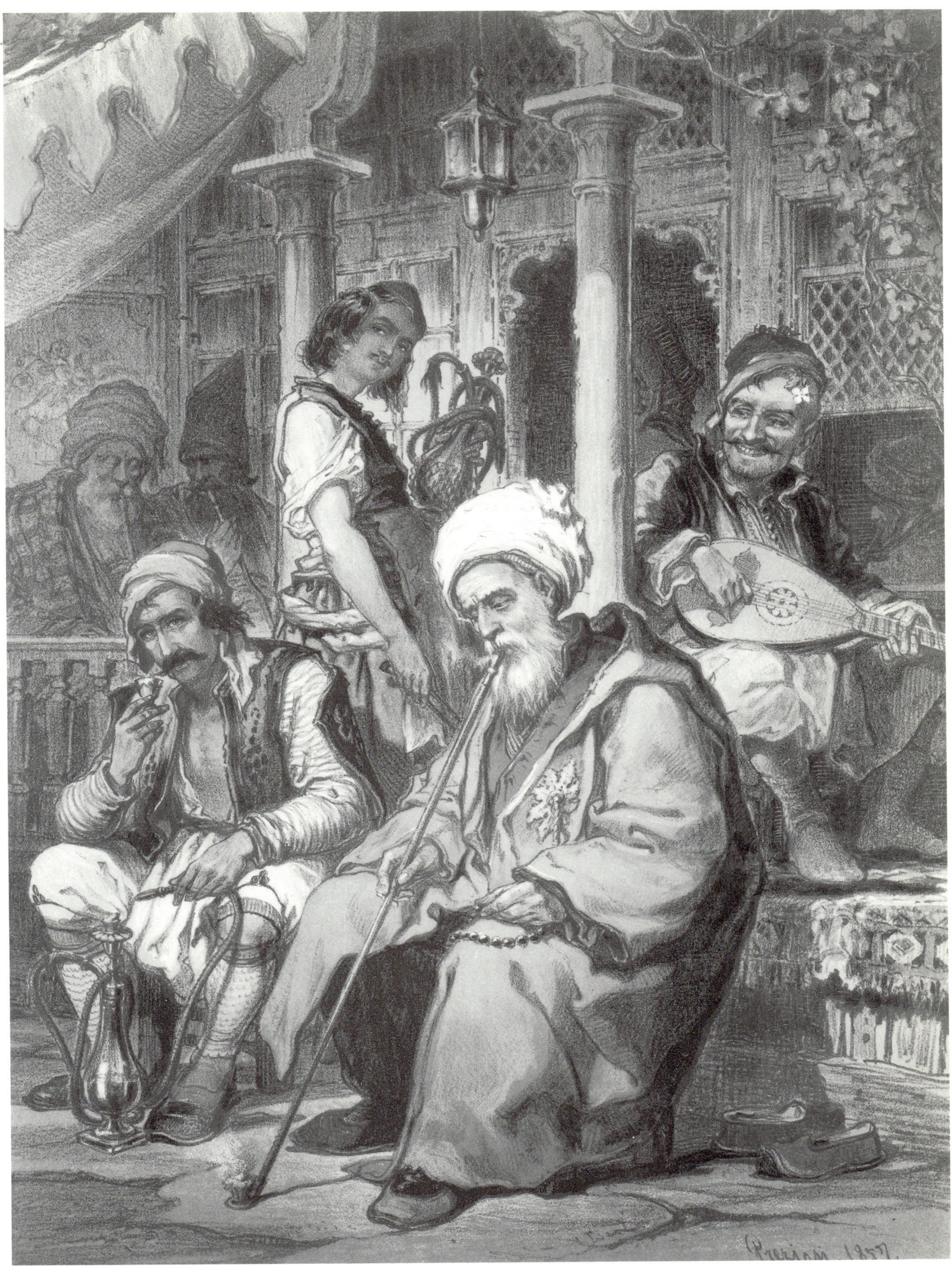

rendering of various races and ranks. Published in Paris, Preziosi's lithographs were intended for a general public whose knowledge of Turkey would have been scanty, and on whom the finesse and innuendo which characterises watercolours such as *A Turkish Coffee-House* would have been lost. He selected, probably with the aid of Lemercier's astute commercial eye, the subjects which would confirm his western European market's idea of the exotic East. They would expect to see beautiful young girls, veiled, but not shrouded in shapeless *feraces*; and they would look for pretty children, leering or avaricious old men, and scruffy, down-at-heel hawkers, but they would not have understood how all these people fitted into their complex society. They would expect evidence of decay and poverty, as long as it remained picturesque and did not become squalid or disturbing. Two decades earlier, Thomas Allom, in his illustrations to Fisher's *Constantinople* (1839) and to *Character and Costume in Turkey and Italy* (c.1840), had appealed to the same popular taste. He too had depicted well-known subjects such as the café, the favourite odalisque and the public scribe. But beside Preziosi's lusty, full-blooded individuals, Allom's appear pale and insipid. Working within the romantic conventions of the early nineteenth century, he softens forms and generalises details of architecture and costume. There is none of the immediacy and robust realism which are the salient characteristics of Preziosi's images. Nor is there the sly humour which to a greater or lesser degree creeps into most of Preziosi's figure compositions. In addition, Allom's printed images are for the most part monochromatic, while Preziosi's are highly coloured. The novelty of Preziosi's strong and sometimes harsh colouring is evident when his lithographs are compared to contemporary books of Turkish costume, such as Jean Brindesi's *Elbicei Attika Musée Des Anciens Costumes Turcs De Constantinople*, also published by Lemercier, c.1855. This differs from Preziosi's album not only in technique but in concept for, like earlier prints and watercolours of Turkish costume, they are concerned with the civil, religious and military officials of the Ottoman establishment rather than with the everyday life of ordinary people. Brindesi's album seems to have been brought out specifically to illustrate the contents of a costume museum which had been recently set up in an old house in the At Meydanı in Constantinople,[20] and which was a manifestation of the nostalgia then being felt by the Franks for obsolete Ottoman traditions. That Preziosi's album was also consciously fixing for posterity images of a culture undergoing an immense transformation, was another reason for its popularity.

19 An Indian from Calcutta 1852

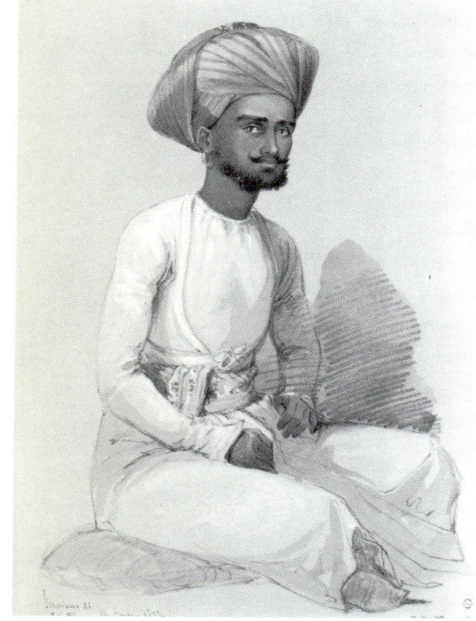

During the 19th century the system of government practised by the Ottoman rulers of the previous four centuries was swept away in favour of a new style of administration imported from the West. The first great reforming Sultan was Mahmud II (1808-39) whose most revolutionary act was the abolition and extermination of the Janissaries in 1826 and the establishment in their stead of an army

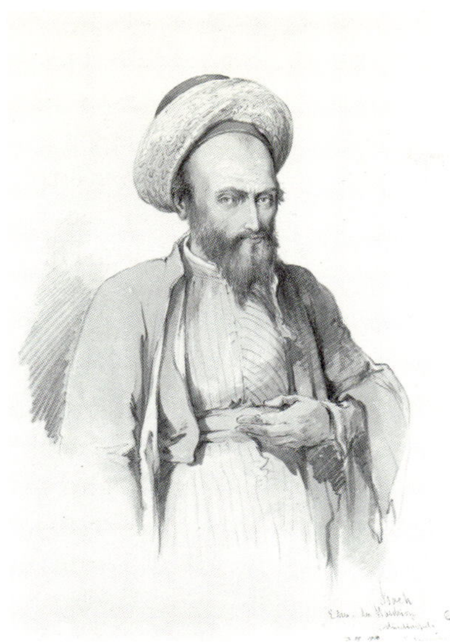

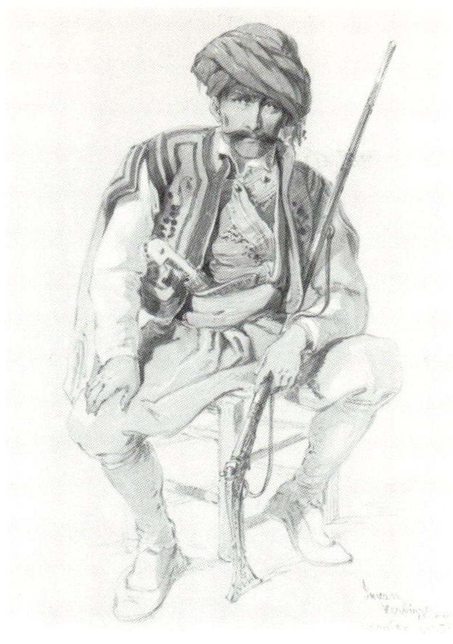

26 Isaac, a Karaite Jew from Hasköy near Constantinople 1852

32 Iuvan Verbizga (?) from Montenegro 1854

structured along western lines and with European-style uniforms. A few years later the clothing reform was extended to civilian officials: the fez replaced the various forms of turban, and trousers, frock-coats and capes were worn instead of robes and slippers. Since dress, and especially headgear, were the means by which a man indicated both his social status and his religious allegiance, these fundamental changes were accepted by the ordinary population only gradually. In addition, a whole series of reforms, collectively known as the Tanzimat or Reorganisation, was put into effect by successive Sultans, and gradually permeated all aspects of Turkish life. Over the years new secular systems of justice, economy and education were established and the supremacy of the *Ulema* (body of religious officials) was eroded. Such changes undermined the whole fabric of Turkish society. In the old order an accepted set of loyalties and obligations had regulated the lives of ordinary people. When a new set of alien institutions, originating in the Christian countries which had long been the enemies of Turkey, were imposed on long established Islamic traditions, a great deal of confusion and resentment ensued. As Théophile Gautier remarked, to 'the old Turks in green caftans and large turbans . . . all the "reformed" ideas are horrible and impious'.[21]

In addition to western dress, western styles of architecture and decoration were also introduced. These were noticeable by the late 1830s, and one of Julia Pardoe's intentions, in *The Beauties of the Bosphorus* was, she declared in the preface, to record not only the traditional customs of the Turks but also the whole aspect of Constantinople and its environs before they disappeared. The Rev. Walsh was equally aware of the changes that were taking place. 'Constantinople, having for centuries exhibited the singular and extraordinary spectacle of a Mahommedan town in a Christian region, and stood still while all about it were advancing in the march

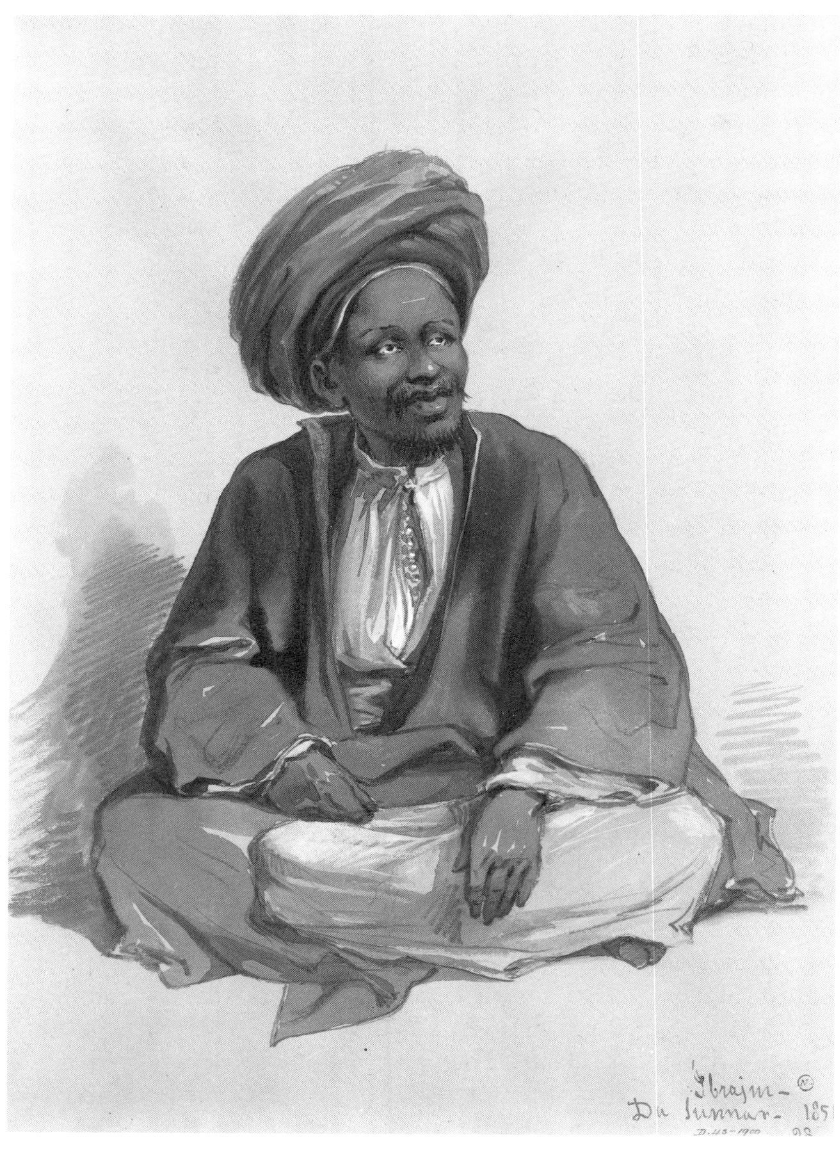

34 Ibrahim, a Muslim from Sennar 1856

of improvement, has at length, as suddenly as unexpectedly, been roused from its slumbering stupidity; the city and its inhabitants are daily undergoing a change as extraordinary as unhoped for; and the present generation will see with astonishment that revolution of usages and opinions, during a single life, which has not happened in any other country in revolving centuries. It is thus that the former state of things is hurrying away, and he who visits the capital to witness the singularities that marked it will be disappointed. It is true it possesses beauties which no revolution of opinions, or changes of events, can alter. Its seven romantic hills, its Golden Horn, its lovely Bosphorus, its exuberant vegetation, its robust and comely people, will still exist;... the taper minaret, the shouting muezzin, the vast cemetery, the gigantic cypress, the snow-white turban, the *beniche* of vivid colours, the feature-covering *yashmak*, the light cáique, the clumsy *arrhuba*, the arched bazaar – all the distinctive peculiarities of a Turkish town – will soon merge into the uniformity of European things and, if the innovation proceeds as rapidly as it has hitherto done, leave scarce a trace behind them'.[22] In their illustrations to these two publications, Allom and Bartlett pictorialised the nostalgia expressed by the two authors.

Not all western observers were sentimental about the processes of reform. William Makepeace Thackeray who spent eight days in Constantinople on his Peninsular and Orient sponsored tour of the Levant in 1844 likened the Sultan, Abdülmecid (1839-61) to 'a young French *roué* worn out by debauch'. While noticing the infiltration of the European spirit and institutions, he also found plenty of evidence of traditional customs: 'I can only say that they (the people) looked to be very good-natured, handsome and lazy; that the women's yellow slippers are very ugly; that the kabobs at the shop hard by the rope bazaar, are very hot and good; and that at the Armenian cook-shops they serve you delicious fish, and a stout raisin wine of no small merit'.[23] The same earthy humour also marks Preziosi's portrayal of Constantinople life. Without sentiment or nostalgia he rendered those aspects of it largely unaffected by progress. In general his subjects are members of the ordinary civilian population of Constantinople dressed in the traditional apparel of their race and class. The exceptions were soldiers and, in the series of lithographs, the *Eunuch of the Seraglio* who wears the *Stambouline* or Frankish frock-coat. (Westerners would have expected to find a black eunuch among a collection of Constantinople 'types' and it would have been anachronistic and inaccurate to have given him the old Ottoman costume of thirty years before.)

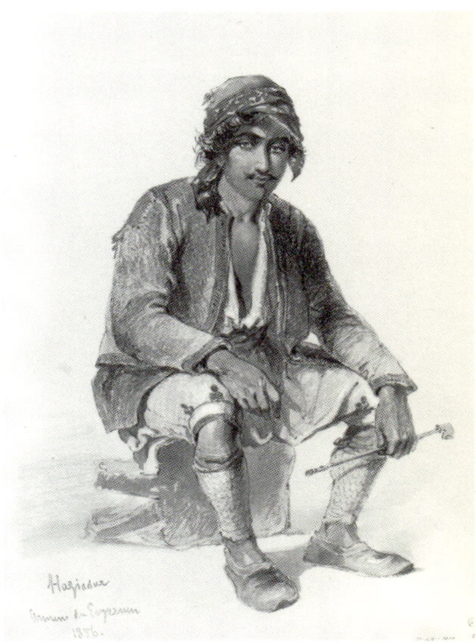

35 Hagiadur, an Armenian from Erzerum 1856

Preziosi's preoccupation with oriental people who remained much as they had done for centuries is especially noticable in an outstanding group of figure studies, also in the Victoria and Albert Museum (cat. no. 15-36). These are thirty-one portraits of men and two women, from different regions of the Ottoman Empire and from countries further East, such as Persia, India and Russia. Once again there is no record of any commission, if indeed there was one. Although the studies are executed on similar types and sizes of paper, they are dated over a period of four years, 1852 to 1856, an unusually long span for a commissioned work. Preziosi's independent means enabled him to work for his own pleasure as well as for commercial gain, and it is possible that he put together this series for himself, collecting exotic individuals much as a lepidopterist might collect rare and colourful butterflies. Roaming the streets and bazaars of the city he would have had ample opportunity to gather into his net all the various types of traders, artisans, tribesmen, religious devotees and travellers from all over the Ottoman Empire and beyond who were drawn to Constantinople by its wealth, fame and beauty. The extraordinary diversity of race, creed and occupation is the keynote of this series of watercolours. They also reflect Preziosi's skills as a documentor of the human kind. That his

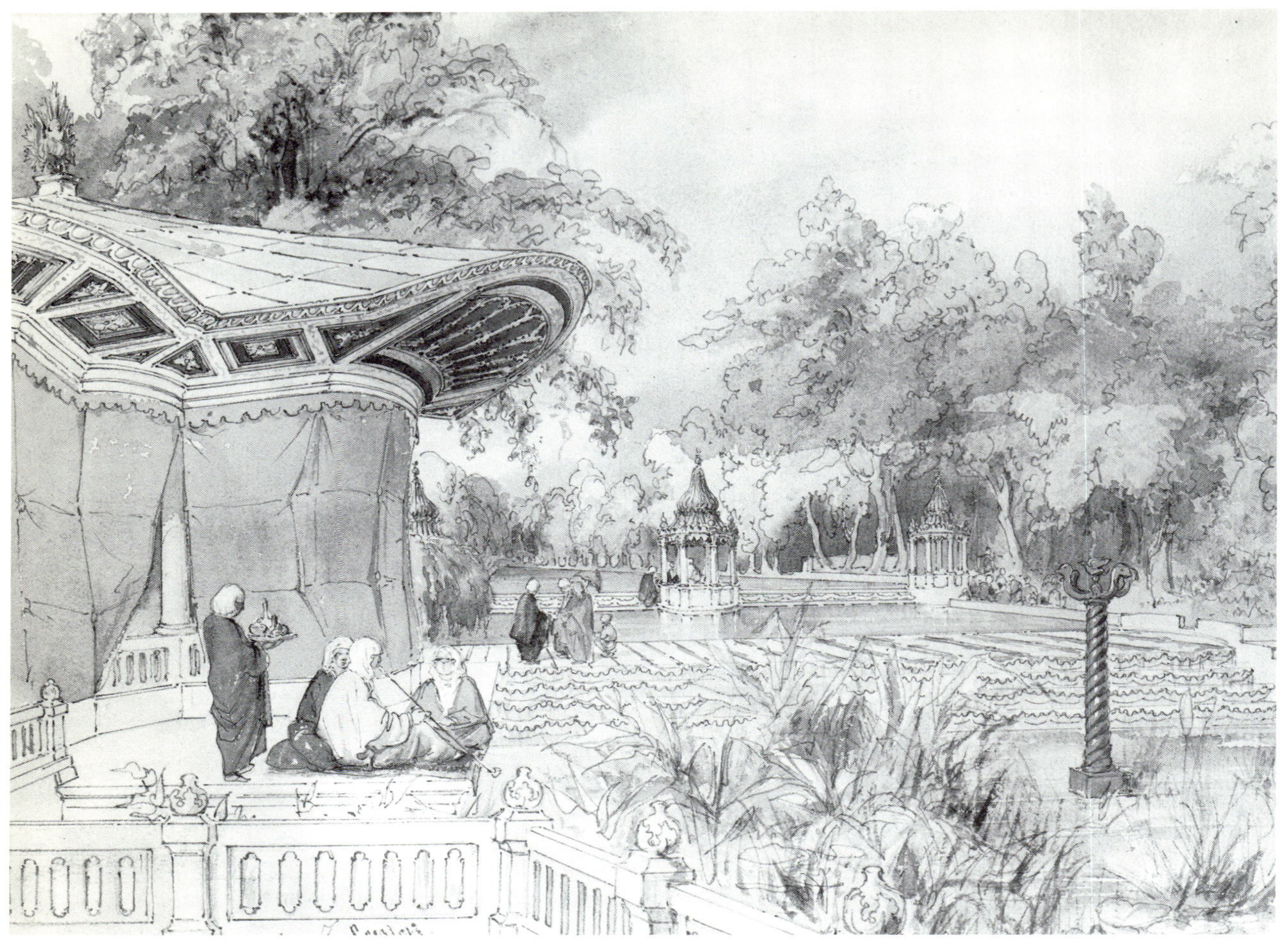

41 The Sweet Waters of Europe c. 1845

subjects appear to have been drawn from life rather than from a hasty sketch or a photograph, suggests that Preziosi had persuaded them to sit for him in his studio in Pera. Each figure is annotated in Preziosi's native Italian with a date and with the identity of the sitter, not only from whence they came but usually what they did, and their names. They are true portraits. Although, like his other figure studies, they represent a particular type of person, they go far beyond this in being first and foremost individuals. Most of the characters whom Preziosi portrayed, many of them from remote regions where foreigners were unknown, would have been inherently suspicious if not hostile to such treatment. Portraiture was a western concept alien to most orientals and especially Muslims who regarded it as sinister and inviting the evil eye.

It is unlikely that Preziosi could have succeeded in this remarkable achievement if he had not been familiar with his subjects' ways and customs and to some extent their common language. Without being able to communicate with them he would not have been able to gain their confidence. Each individual is rendered with extreme sensitivity to the nuances of his character and race: the cunning of the Babylonian with hooded eyes (cat. no. 27), the athletic strength of the handsome Kurd (cat. no. 16), the modest dignity of the Turkish woman (cat. no. 28); the rugged visage and tattered clothes of the old Bulgarian (cat. no. 29), and, by contrast, the complacency and rich garments of the Greek from Antioch (cat. no. 23); the otherworldly gaze of the Indian dervish from Lucknow (cat. no. 18) and the extreme worldliness of the dervish from Bosnia with his elaborate turban, fur-edged robe and roguish grin (cat. no. 36); the fair beard and blue eyes of the Muslim of Batum in Lazistan (cat. no. 22) and the swarthy, smiling, Muslim from Sennar in the Sudan (cat. no. 34). Unlike the artist's more ordinary 'types' these people are shown out of their natural environment, with a consequent focus on their costumes and physiognomies.

These, by any standards, an exceptional group of portraits, are among Preziosi's finest works. They reveal not only his acute observation of his sitters and his knowledge of their cultures, but also the rapidity and assurance with which he could draw. The forms are deftly outlined with pencil or pen and ink, and then given substance with broad sweeps of watercolour, sometimes thickened with bodycolour; details of features and costume are accurately rendered with swift flicks of the brush. Preziosi's sympathetic representation of exotic people invites comparison with that of his better-known, British contemporary, John Frederick Lewis (1805-76). Although different in technique, Preziosi's portraits display the same unpatronising attitude to his subjects as the sketches made by Lewis in Turkey and Egypt during the 1840s.[24] In these works neither artist makes concessions to western taste and each portrays his sitters as human beings of flesh and blood rather than as stylised characters from *The Arabian Nights*.

The places of Constantinople attracted the same discerning treatment from Preziosi as its people. Once again the well-known views across the Bosphorus, the Golden Horn, the Sweet Waters of

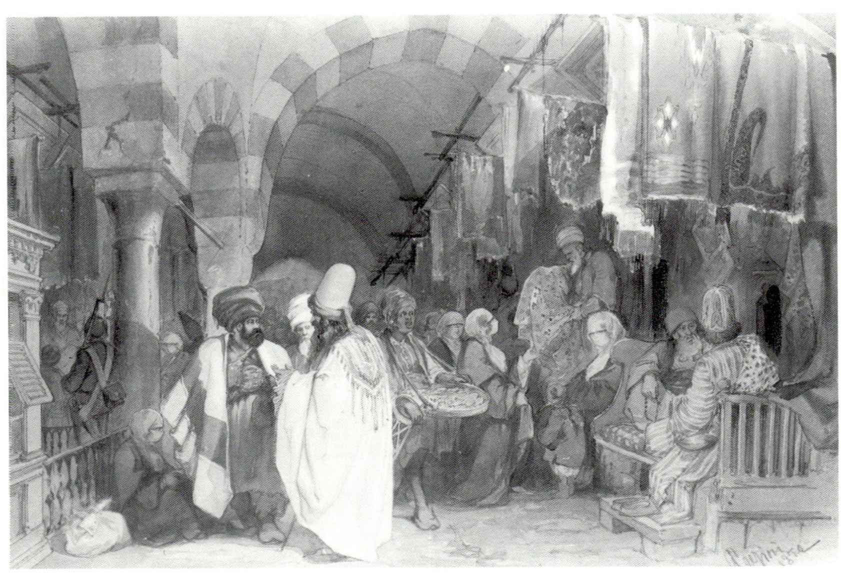

44 The Sandal Bedesteni or Silk Market 1852

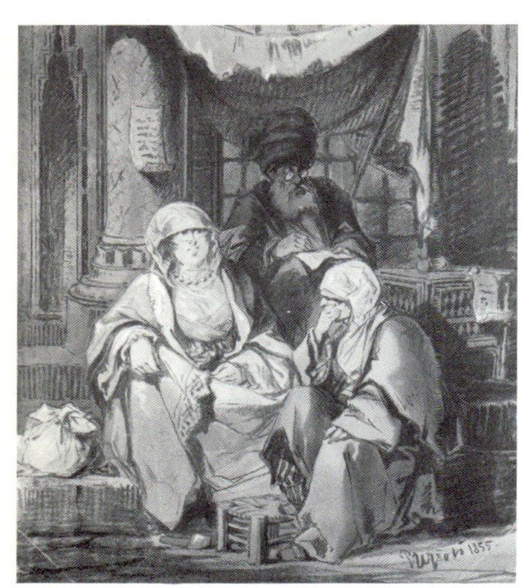

49 The Turkish Letter-Writer or *Arzuhaici* 1855

Asia and of Europe, as well as of the cemeteries, streets, bazaars and cafés, bear the stamp of his individuality. Preziosi differed from other artists such as Bartlett who illustrated these scenes, because he was independent by nature and had an unusual background and training. He could break out of the mould of picturesque topography and create compositions to suit his subject-matter rather than vice versa. He emphasised the natural picturesque qualities of his scenes – the mêlée of women, *kayıks* and *arabas* at the Sweet Waters of Europe (cat. no. 48); the swelling curves of a kiosk beside the cascades at the same location (cat. no. 41); ramshackle market stalls overflowing with exotic merchandise (cat. no. 44);[25] boats of every shape and size which ply the entrance to the Golden Horn (cat. no. 45).

Preziosi seems to have been at his most active in Constantinople during the 1850s, the decade to which several of his views are dated. However, a large number of views have no dates, and since he appears to have adopted a variety of styles simultaneously, his work is difficult to place chronologically. In general, his very early scenes tend to be schematic, giving place to the assurance and greater complexity of his mature years, and later to some elaborate, highly wrought watercolours.[26]

During the 1850s, a major international event – the Crimean War – invested his views of Constantinople with even greater interest. The number of visitors, both military and civilian, rose enormously, and consequently the demand for pictorial mementoes of the scenery. Several of Preziosi's landscapes at this time include evidence of the war – soldiers, the allied fleets anchored in the Bosphorus, or the Christian cemetery at Scutari (cat. nos. 47 and 51)[27] Information about the war area was so eagerly received in Britain that the *Illustrated London News* sent special artists and reporters to observe not only the scene of the action but also the people and places of the Turkish capital city. As early as 1850 Constantinople was described as 'a focus of extraordinary interest'[28] and, at the height of the war, at least a dozen issues of the periodical described and illustrated aspects of Constantinople life as well as events more closely related to the war. The issue of 24 September 1853 carried a sixteen page special supplement on the Ottoman Empire and the following year an occasional series, 'Sketches in Turkey' included street scenes, a coffee-seller, a school and an inn.[29] The artist sent out by the *ILN* to draw these scenes, identified only as 'G', may well have been inspired by Preziosi's watercolours. If Preziosi was directly involved in any *ILN* illustrations at this time he was not acknowledged. It was not until 1859 that a wood-engraving of the banquet held at the British Embassy to commemorate Queen Victoria's birthday was credited as 'from a drawing by M. Preziosi, the well-known artist of Oriental subjects'.[30] This and watercolours such as *The British Embassy Summer Residence, Therapia* are further evidence of Preziosi's continuing associations with the British diplomatic community.[31]

In 1870 the *ILN* devoted a whole page of its issue for 2 July to a wood-engraving of a *View of the Ruins after the Great Fire at Constantinople* after 'a sketch by M. Preziosi, an accomplished artist well known to all residents and visitors in that city, which shows the aspect of the ruins around the palace of the British Embassy, with the forlorn groups of distressed people searching for the dead bodies of their friends'.[32] This, one of the worst of the many fires which almost daily afflicted Constantinople, had recently destroyed much of the Christian quarter of Pera, including the British Embassy.

These two *ILN* illustrations are examples of Preziosi's more elaborate compositions depicting specific events instead of his more usual scenes of everyday life and landscape. Also in this category are his views of the ceremonies surrounding the voyages of the Sultan's barges to and from the numerous palaces and mosques on the Bosphorus, for example the Nusretiye Camii (cat. no. 39)[33]. Similar scenes, dated 1865, were purchased by the Prince of Wales, who visited Preziosi's Pera studio on 8 April 1869.[34]

Although he continued to paint Constantinople scenes during the 1860s, Preziosi also spent time in this decade travelling. Constantinople was no longer a 'focus of extraordinary interest' to western Europeans and this may have contributed to his decision to widen his repertoire of subjects. In 1862 he accompanied H.C. du Bois, envoy extraordinary from the Netherlands to the Ottoman court, to Egypt. One of the places they visited on the way was Beirut, as is recorded by a colourful and animated watercolour of the harbour with a small boat ferrying passengers, including soldiers, possibly to a larger ship at anchor further out.[35] In Cairo, another cosmopolitan

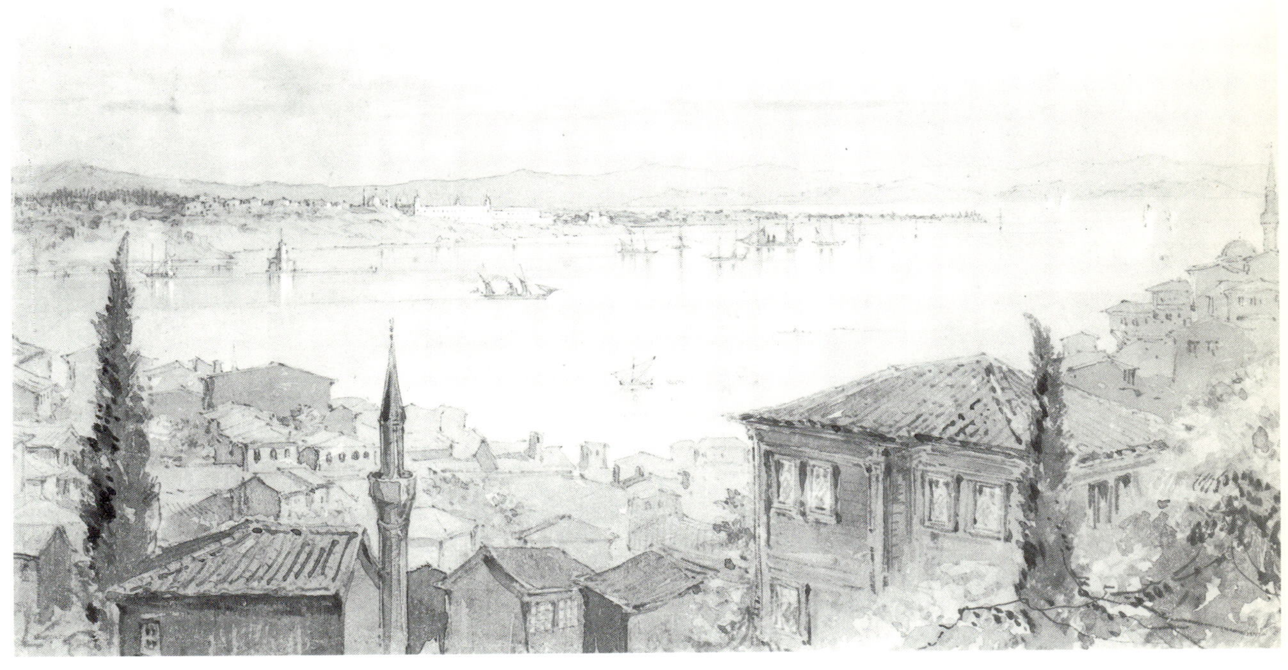

50 A View across the Bosphorus c. 1855-60

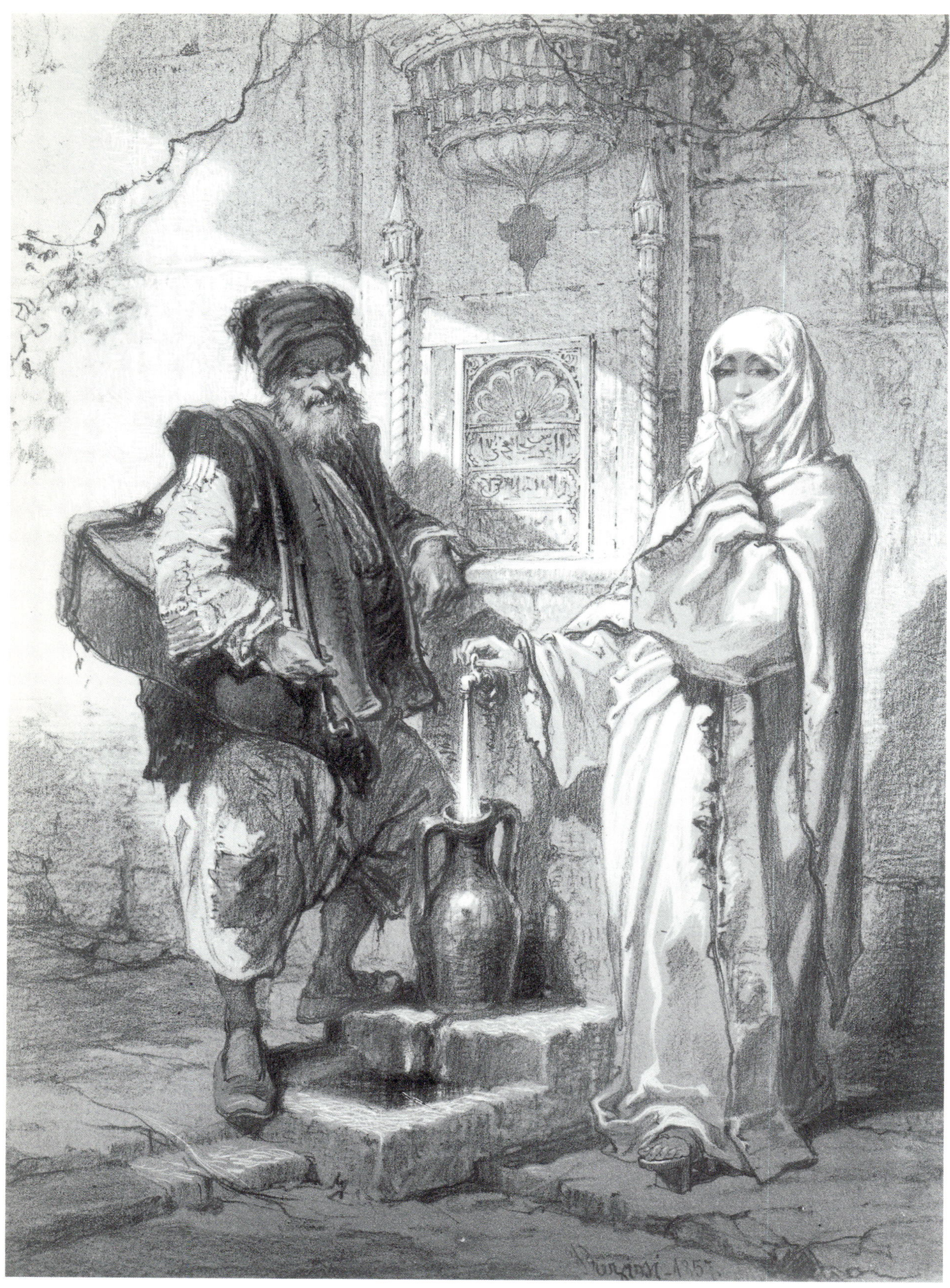

eastern capital, Preziosi studied the ordinary people, just as he had done in Constantinople, gathering together material for a publication similar in kind to *Stamboul*. Entitled *Souvenirs du Caire* and dedicated to his travelling companion, its everyday life subjects include a street barber, dancing almahs, camel drivers, dervishes and Coptic women. As before, the simplification of character, bold outlines and strong colours were intended to make images easy for westerners to assimilate. Again Preziosi was his own lithographer and the plates were printed in Paris by Lemercier, probably in 1863, using the same methods as before.

Preziosi may also have travelled to England from Paris, since in 1863 he exhibited an Egyptian subject, *Sunset on the Banks of the Nile*, at the Royal Academy.[36] Later in the same decade his work was included in the Turkish Pavilion at the Paris International Exhibition of 1867.

Towards the end of the 1860s Preziosi discovered a new range of subjects, though still within his habitual theme of the life and customs of commoners. During the consecutive summers of 1868 and 1869 he visited Rumania twice, spending most of the time in Bucharest but also travelling through the countryside. It has been suggested that the two trips were undertaken at the behest of the new reigning Prince, Charles I, who may have been introduced to Preziosi on a visit to Constantinople in 1866, and who wanted a pictorial record of his state tours. Accounts of the many fine sketches and finished watercolours which derive from these journeys are published elsewhere.[37] Their chief characteristics are, as with all his best work, variety, vitality and sensitivity. The watercolours represent an aspect of Rumanian folk or religious life, very often a market or a fair, or people gathered round a church or monastery. Once again, Preziosi's sympathy with his subject matter is strikingly apparent: he extracts the pictureseque qualities from each scene but does not sentimentalise them. As in his Constantinople scenes, his figures are not cardboard cutouts but full of vim and vigour. His skills in rendering the intricate decorative details of Rumanian architecture are also seen here to great advantage. His landscapes are no mere backdrops, and he is as sensitive in his observation of atmospheric conditions as of the human character.

Little is known of Preziosi's activities during the last decade of his life. His home was now in Yeşilköy, a quiet village on the outskirts of Constantinople.[38] He maintained his studio in Pera, however, and his contacts with foreign and native city life. According to family tradition he became a court painter to the Sultan Abdul Hamid II (1876-1909). Few works from these years appear to survive, although his obituary mentions some late 'canvases' of high quality.[39] Murray's *Turkey* makes clear that photographers had largely usurped the role of artists as the purveyors of Constantinople imagery to the tourists; for although the guide recommended the 'coloured sketches by Mr. Preziosi', it deemed a photograph by Messrs. Abdullah Brothers 'one of the most valuable curiosities

Opposite:

52 A Water-Carrier or *Saka* and a Woman at a *Sebil* c. 1857

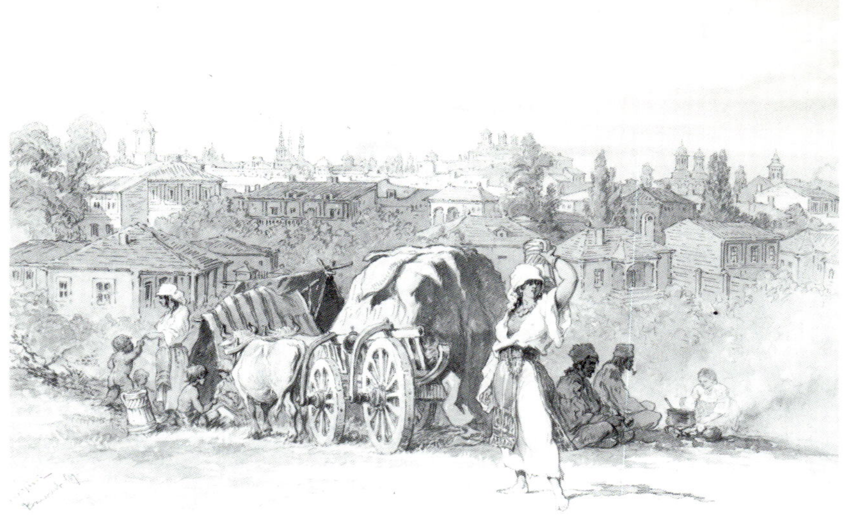

53 A Gipsy Encampment outside Bucharest 1869

that can be carried away from the capital of Turkey'.[40]

Preziosi's death was announced in the *Eastern Express* (continuation of the *Levant Herald*), a recently established English language newspaper. On 27 September this reported that while out hunting near Yeşilköy his gun accidentally went off, mortally wounding him; he died the following day. His many admirers from both the Frankish and Turkish communities of Constantinople followed his funeral cortège to the Catholic cemetery of San Stefano. An obituary, written in French, in the same newspaper, on 29 September, wrote highly both of his work and his reputation. 'Il avait tant de naturel dans ses croquis, le dessin et le coloris en était si parfaits, la verité du sujet que l'artiste voulait representer était si saisissante, que tous les voyageurs venant à Constantinople ne manquaient pas visiter son atelier et d'acheter ses croquis qui ont ainsi acquis une renommée universelle.' His character too was praised as 'élevé, plein d'energie, aiment les arts jusqu'à l'enthousiasme, il était aimé de tous ceux qui approchaient. Il était sincère et modeste'. It seems that without the constraints imposed by the need either to make a living or an academic reputation, Preziosi was free to follow his own artistic inclinations. His enthusiasm for his painting and his subjects is reflected in the natural spontaneity and vigour of his work. He was, as his obituarist states, 'Facile Princeps dans sa specialité'.

Notes to the Text

1 Julia Pardoe, *The City of the Sultan and Domestic Manners of the Turks*, 2nd. edn. London, Vol. I, 1838, p.82.

2 *Illustrated London News*, 16 July 1859, p.51; John Murray (pub.), *A Handbook for Travellers in Turkey and Asia, including Constantinople, the Bosphorus, Dardanelles, Brousa and Plain of Troy*, new ed. revised, London, 1871, p.118.

3 Adolphe Thalasso, *L'art ottoman. les peintres de Turquie*, Paris, 1911, p.11.

4 See bibliography; several of these sources include information obtained from the Preziosi family in Malta.

5 Frank (Turkish *efrenc*) was the name adopted by Muslims of the Near East for Christians.

6 William Howard Russell, *A Diary in the East during the tour of the Prince and Princess of Wales*, London, 1869, Vol. 2, p.507. A photograph of Preziosi in his 'charming rooms' confirms Russell's description (reproduced on the back cover of Ondeş *op. cit.*).

7 Works by both these artists are in the Searight Collection.

8 Julia Pardoe, *The Beauties of the Bosphorus*, London, 1837-39, part 1, pp.3-4.

9 Murray, *op.cit.*, p.63; quoting from Thomas Hope, *Anastasius: or, Memoirs of a Greek*, London, 1819.

10 Alexander Kinglake, *Eothen*, 2nd. edn. London, 1845, p.41.

11 *Julia Pardoe*, 1838, *op.cit.*, p.85.

12 Sold Christie's 17.3.1983, lot 170. The *Eastern Express* (*Levant Herald*) obituary, 29 September 1882, gives 1840 as the date of his arrival, but this may not be correct.

13 *Dictionary of National Biography*.

14 For the Curzon album, *Costumes of Constantinople*, 1844, see catalogue nos. 1-14; British Museum, Prints and Drawings Department, 197 b 15. Ten of these were engraved in Curzon's well-known, *Visits to Monasteries in the Levant*, London, 1849; in the explanatory note to the list of illustrations he states: 'The costumes are from drawings made in Constantinople by a Maltese artist. They are all portraits, and represent the costumes worn at the present day in different parts of the Turkish Empire'.

15 *A Greek Woman*, dated *1843*; *A Turk of the Middle Class*, dated *15 Janvier '43*; *A Soldier*, dated *17 Septem. 1843*.

16 Austen Henry Layard, *Early Adventures in Persia, Susiana and Babylonia, including a residence among the Bakhtiyari and other wild tribes before the discovery of Nineveh*, London, 1887, Vol.I. The drawing is in the British Museum, Department of Western Asiatic Antiquities, 1976-9-25-9.

17 Their names were Mathilde, Giulia, Catherine, and Roberto; descendents still live in Turkey. A signed drawing by Mathilde is in the Collection of H.M. the Queen.

18 This is according to the Marquis of Ruvigny's *Titled Nobility of Europe*, 1914.

19 These are in the Searight Collection.

20 Théophile Gautier's, *Constantinople of Today*, London, 1854 (translated from the French), includes a chapter on the museum (XXVI, pp.319-26).

21 Gautier, *op.cit.*, p.262.

22 Rev. Robert Walsh, *Constantinople and the Scenery of the Seven Churches of Asia Minor*, London, 1839, Vol. I, preface.

23 M.A. Titmarsh [William Makepeace Thackeray], *Notes of a Journey from Cornhill to Cairo*, London, 1845, p.99; chapter VII is devoted to his visit to Constantinople.

24 On Lewis see, Major-General J.M. Lewis CBE, *John Frederick Lewis RA*, Leigh-on-Sea, 1978.

25 *A Bazaar in Constantinople*, dated 1850, sold Sotheby's 1.6.1983, lot 216; *A Turkish Bazaar*, dated 1853, sold Christie's 29.11.84, lot 183.

26 See catalogue entries; also *A Turkish Bazaar*, dated 1867, sold Christie's 29.11.84, lot 181.

27 Other examples are *The Allied Fleets anchored in the Bosphorus*, dated 1853 and *Encampment at Scutari on the Bosphorus*, dated 11 March 1854, both Government Art Collection, 1806 and 1809.

28 *Illustrated London News*, 16 March 1850, p.170.

29 *Illustrated London News*, January-July 1854, pp.69, 137-8, 285, 301 etc.

30 *Illustrated London News*, 16 July 1859, p.51.

31 Sold Christie's 25.11.82, lot 171.

32 *Illustrated London News*, 2 July 1870, pp.19-20.

33 Also *The Royal Barge on the way to Ortaköy*, Deniz Müsezi (Naval Museum), Istanbul; illustrated in colour in Gülseren Ramazanoğlu, 'A Maltese Painter in love with Istanbul. Amadeo Preziosi', in *Hilton International Istanbul Magazine*, Fall, 1975, pp.8-9.

34 See note 6; the Prince of Wales may also have met Preziosi on his earlier visit in May 1862, when he bought *Stamboul* and possibly other works by the artist. There are several works by Preziosi in the Collection of H.M. the Queen: information kindly supplied by Lady Millar.

35 *Beirut from the Sea*, dated 1862; formerly with Eyre and Hobhouse Limited.

36 R.A. 1863, no.770; Preziosi's address was given as c/o H. Grissell, Esq., The Five Houses, Clapton.

37 See Busuioceanu, 1935 and Nicolau-Golfin, 1976, *op.cit.* in bibliography. The drawings are now in the Muzeul de artă al Republich Socialiste România.

38 According to Ramazanoglu, *op.cit.*, his house there still survives, lived in by a descendent. His obituary (*op.cit.* n.12) writes of the physical sufferings and misfortunes of his last years.

39 *Eastern Express*, *op.cit.*

40 Murray, *op.cit.*, p.118.

The Plates

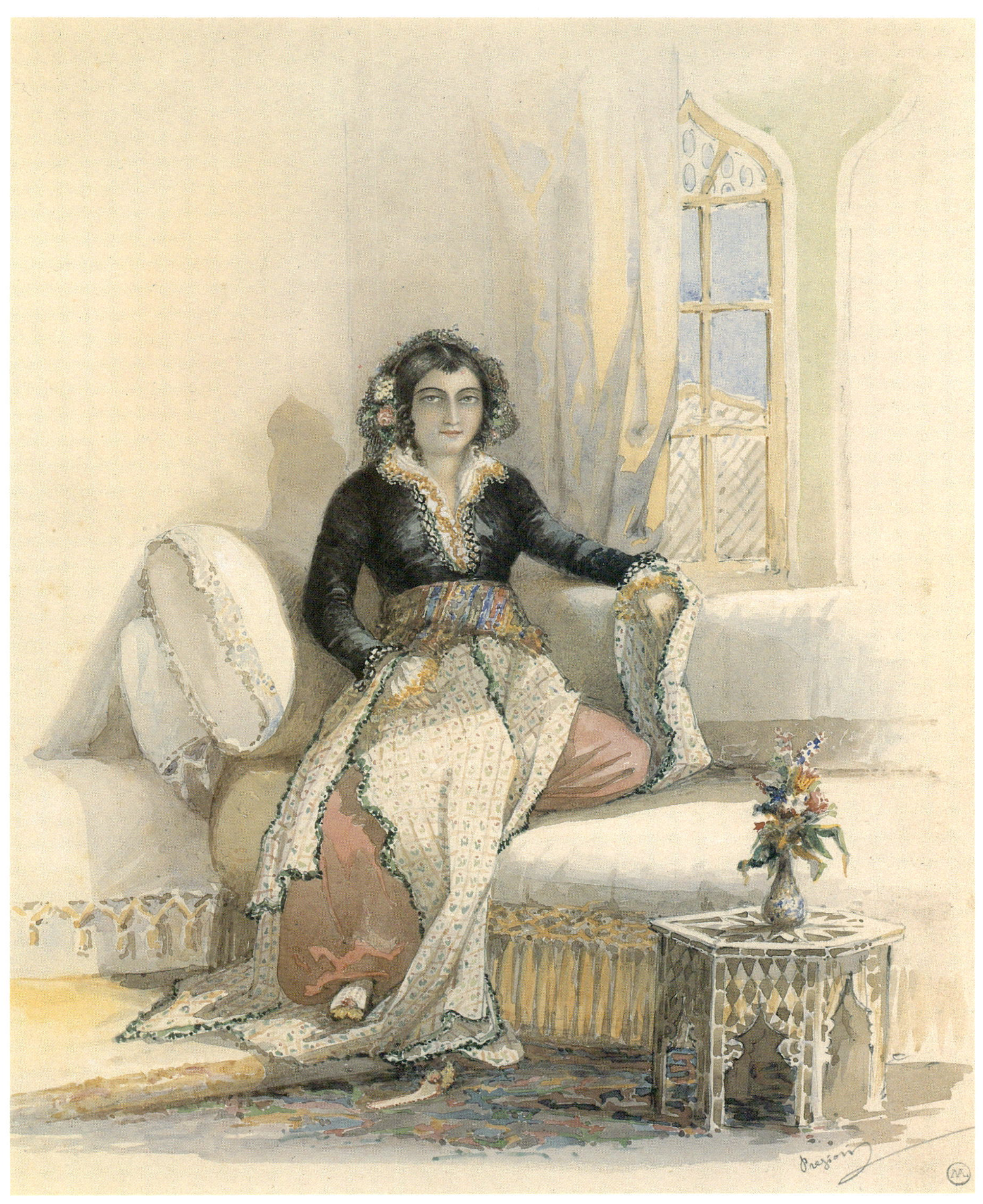

2 Portrait of a woman c. 1843

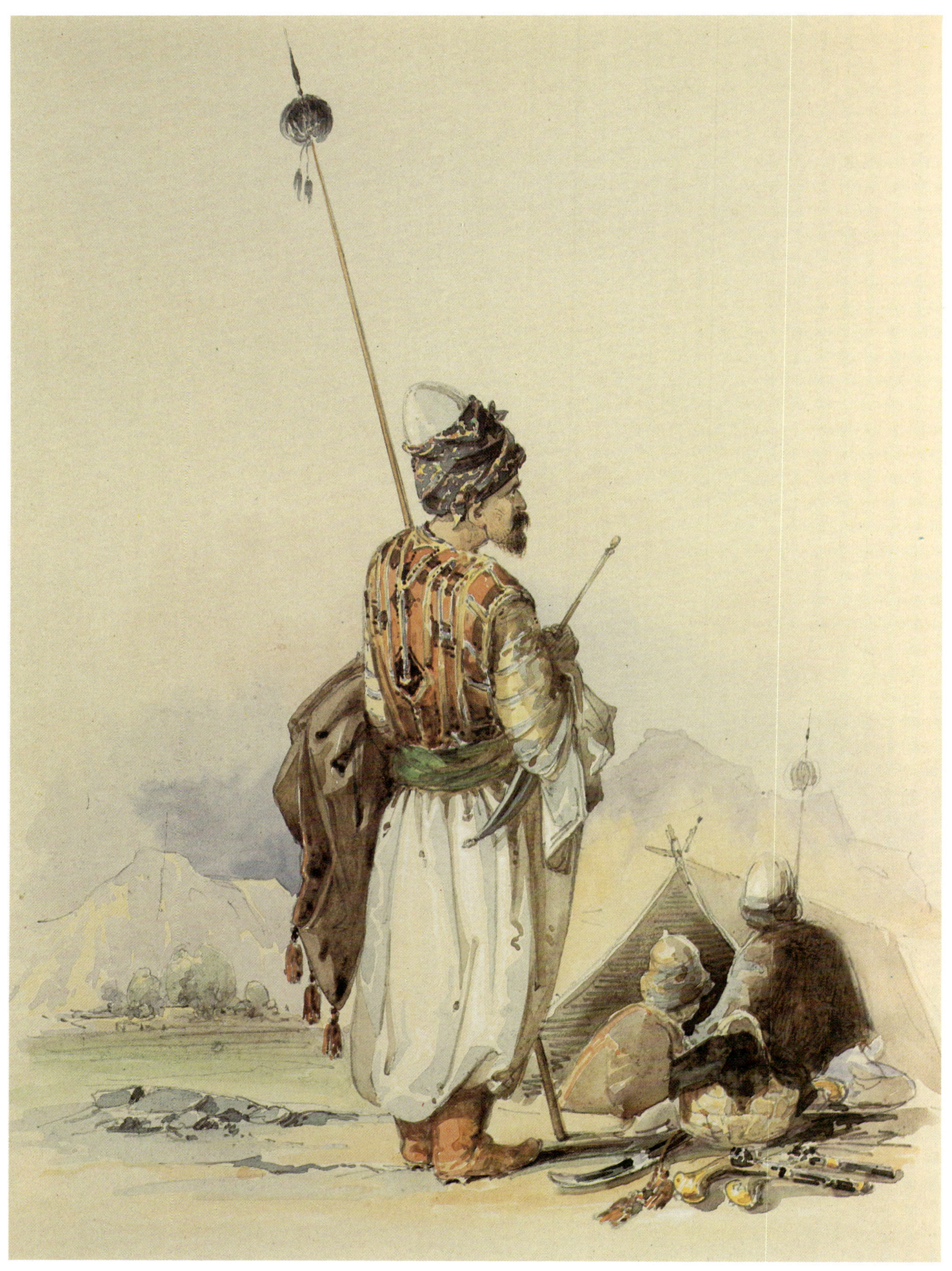

5 A Kurdish Warrior from the Region of Lake Van c. 1843

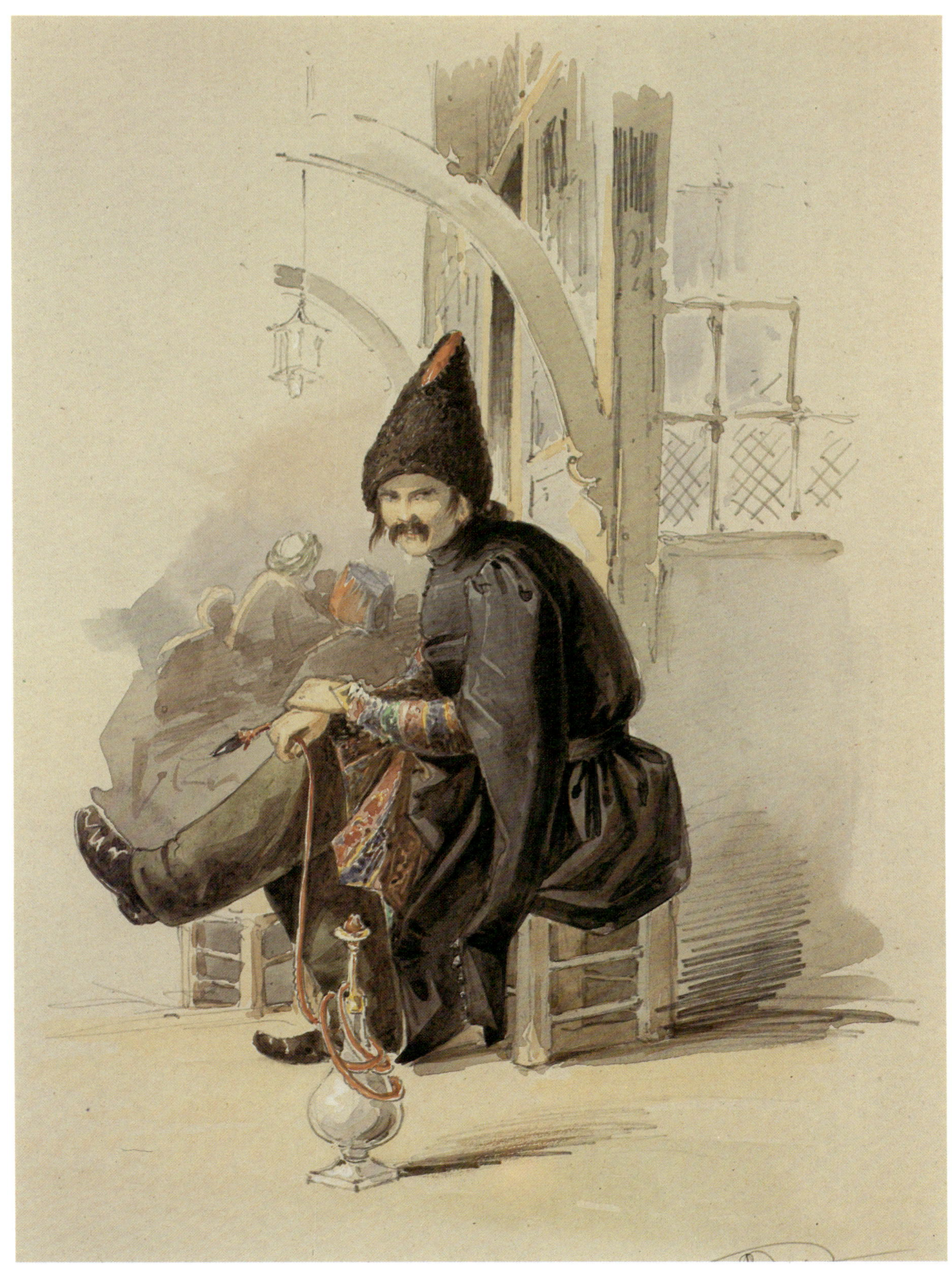

6 A Persian in a Coffee-House c. 1843

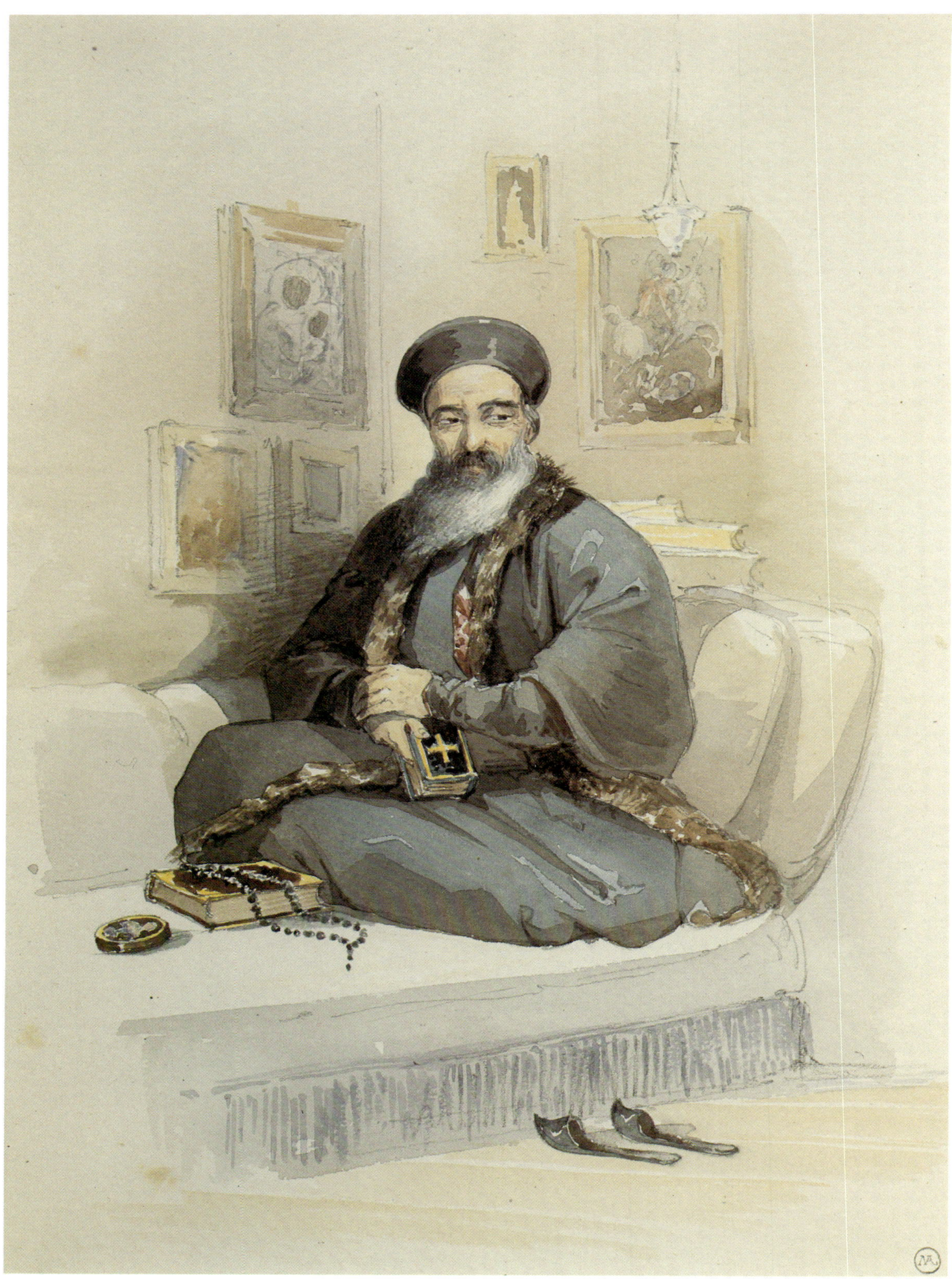

9 A Greek Priest c. 1843

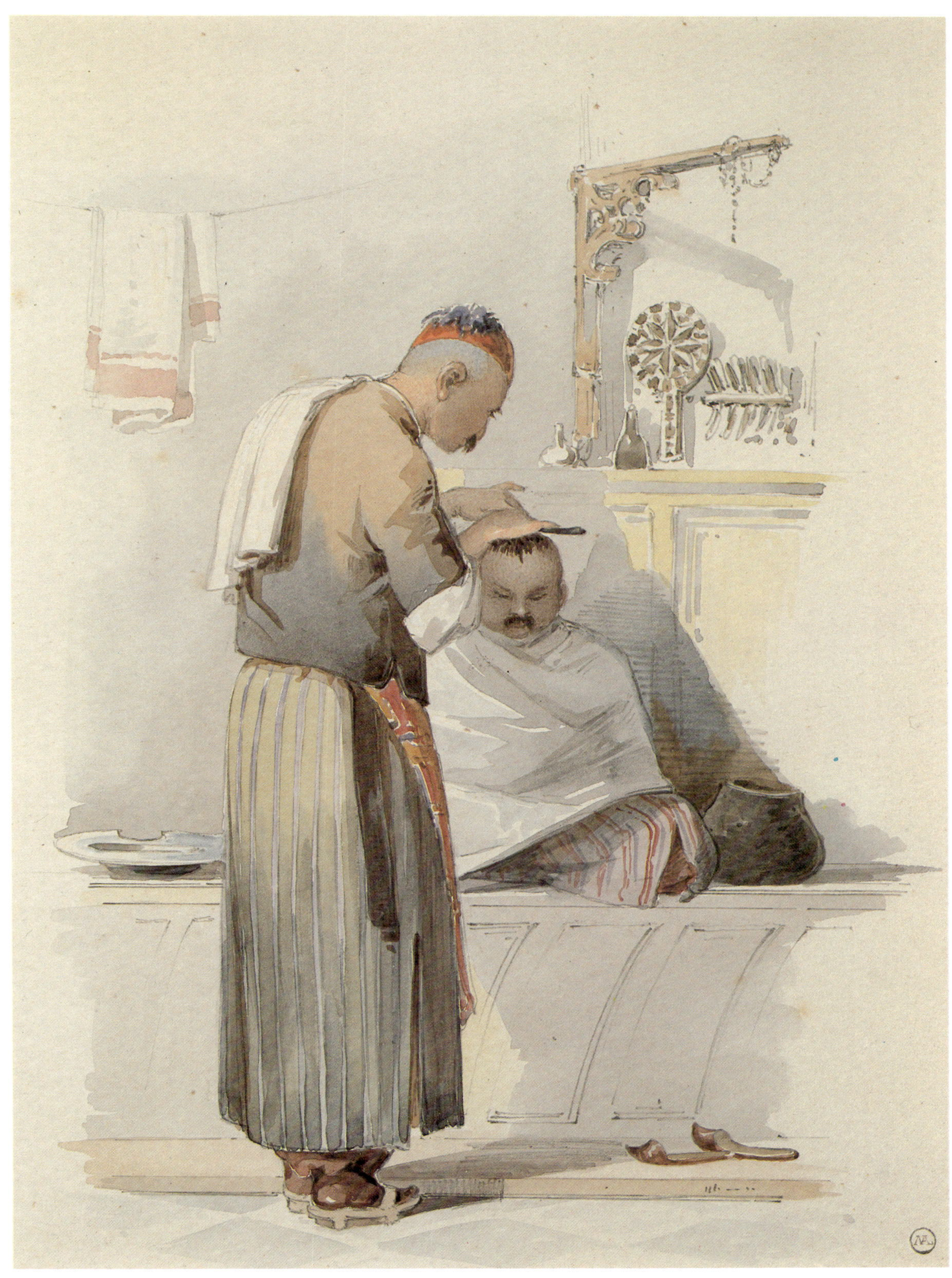

10 A Barber c. 1843

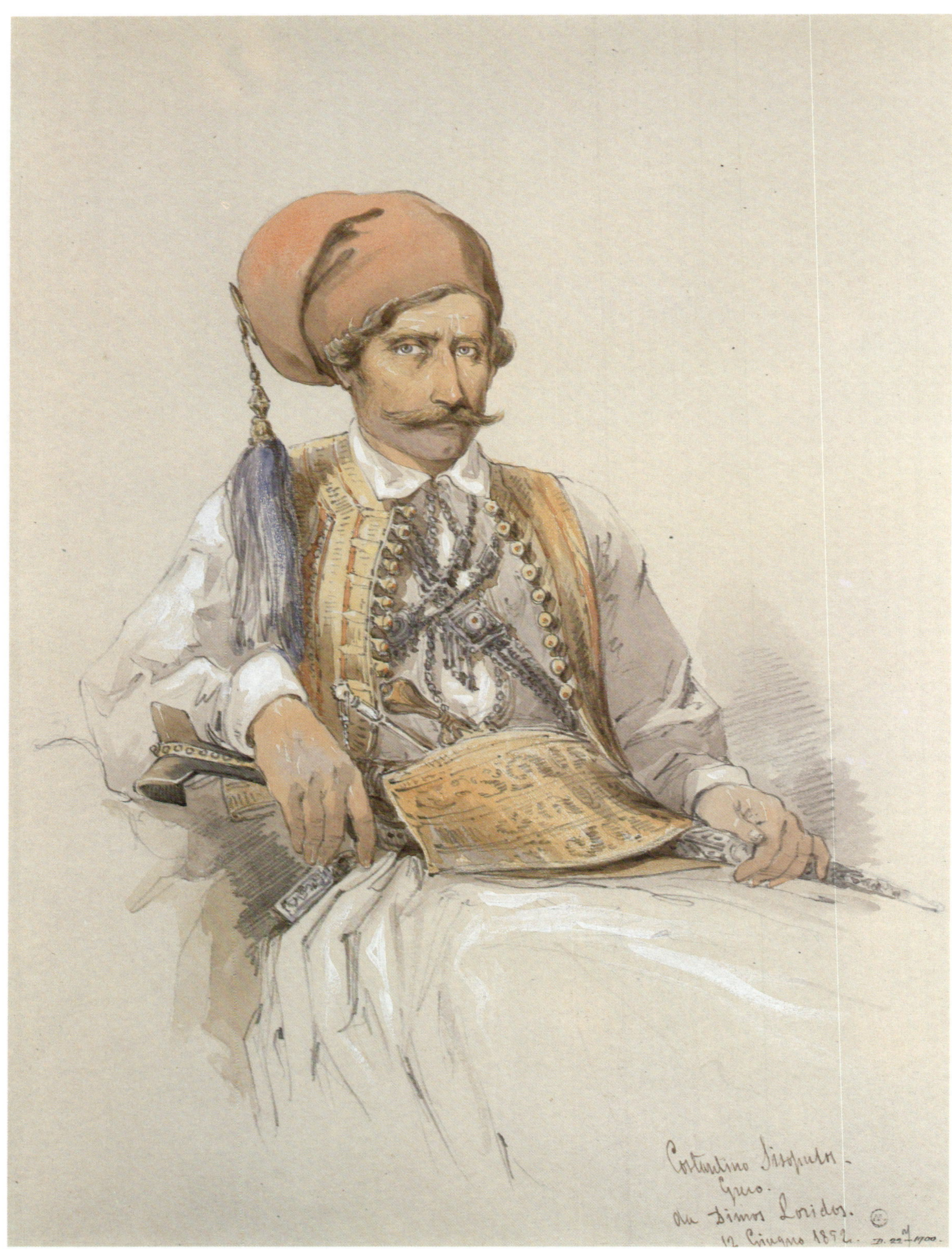

20 Constantino Sisopulos, a Greek from the district of Lokris 1852

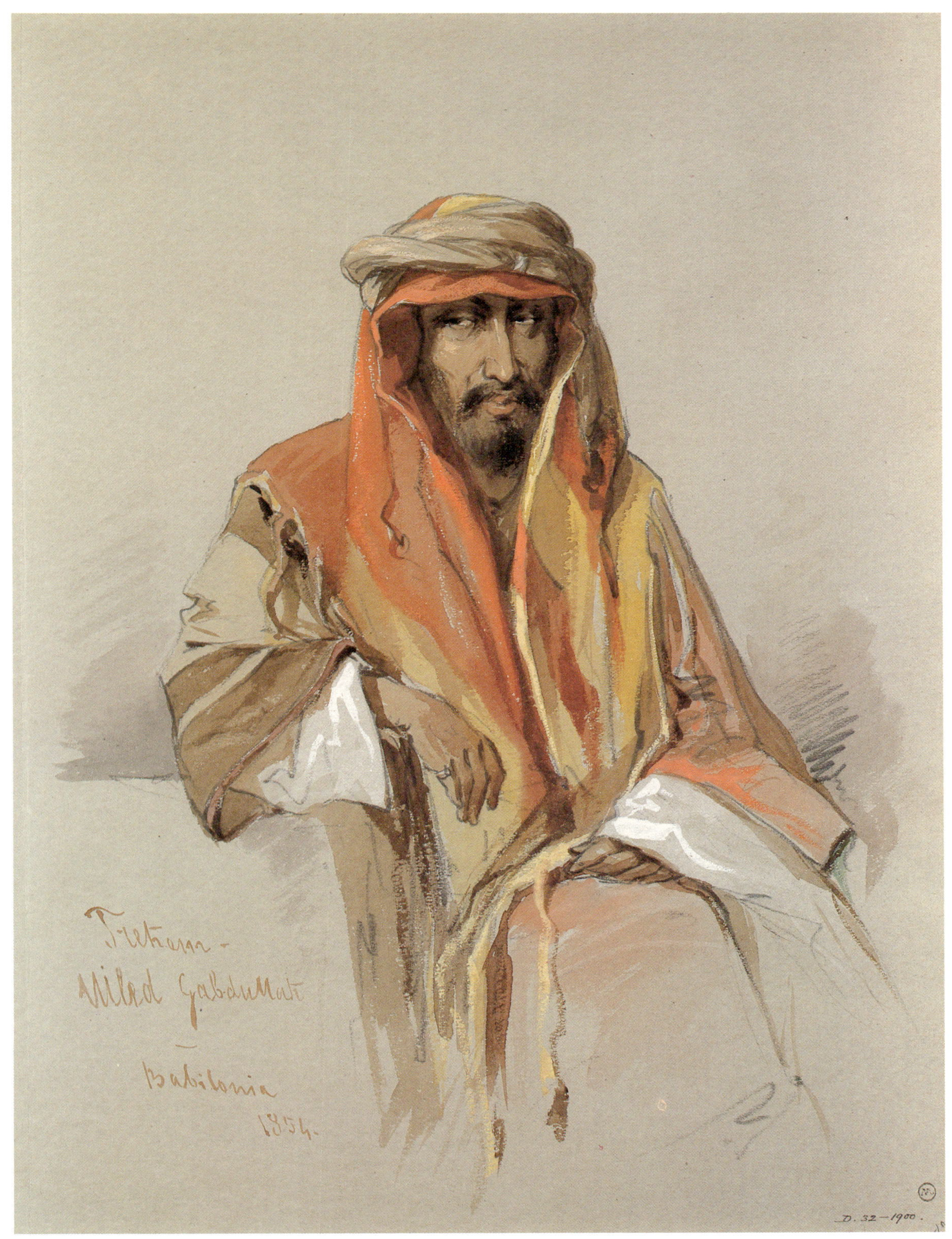

27 Trehem (?) Walid 'Abdullah, an Arab from Iraq 1854

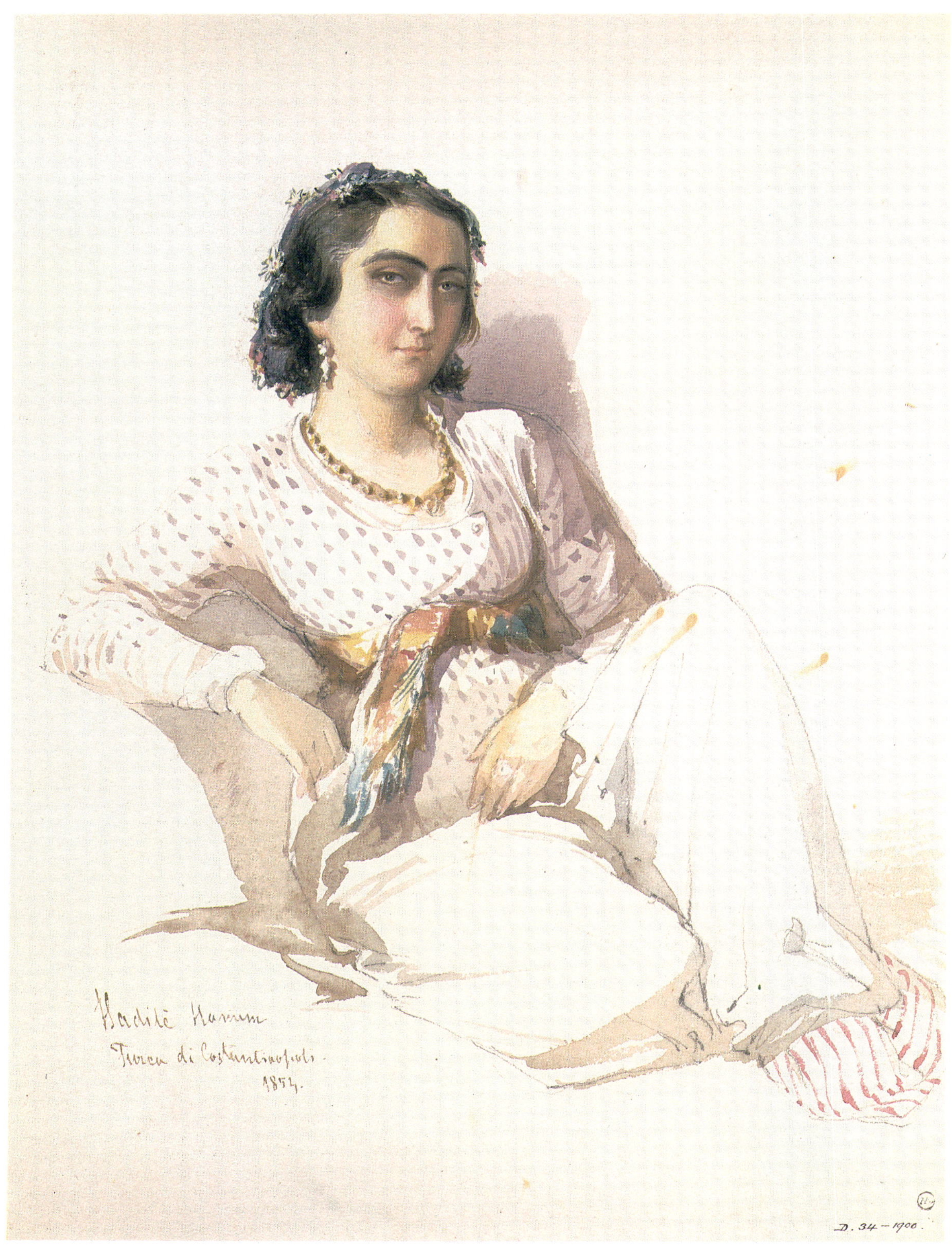

29 Âdile Hanım, a Turkish woman from Constantinople 1854

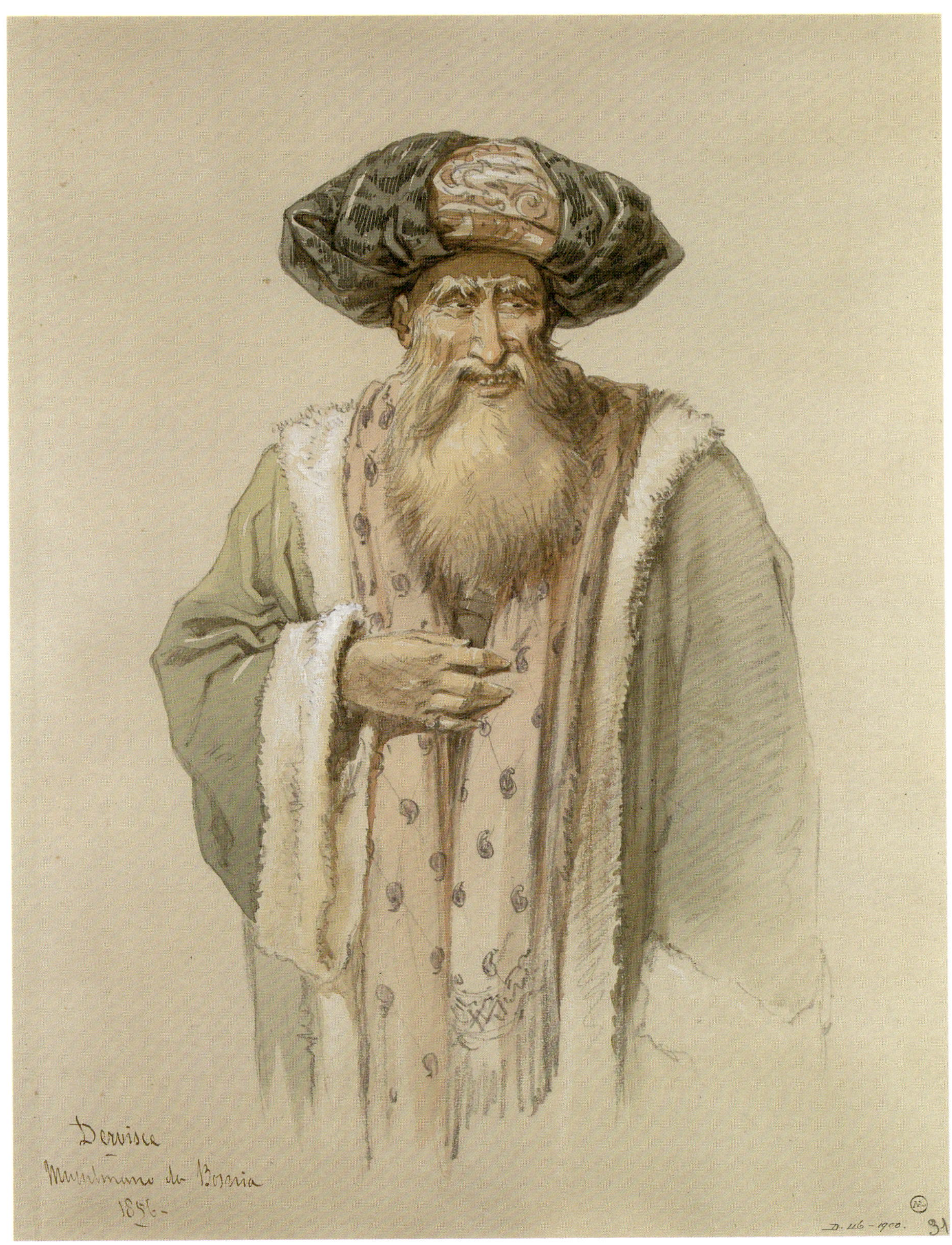

36 A Bektaşi Dervish from Bosnia 1856

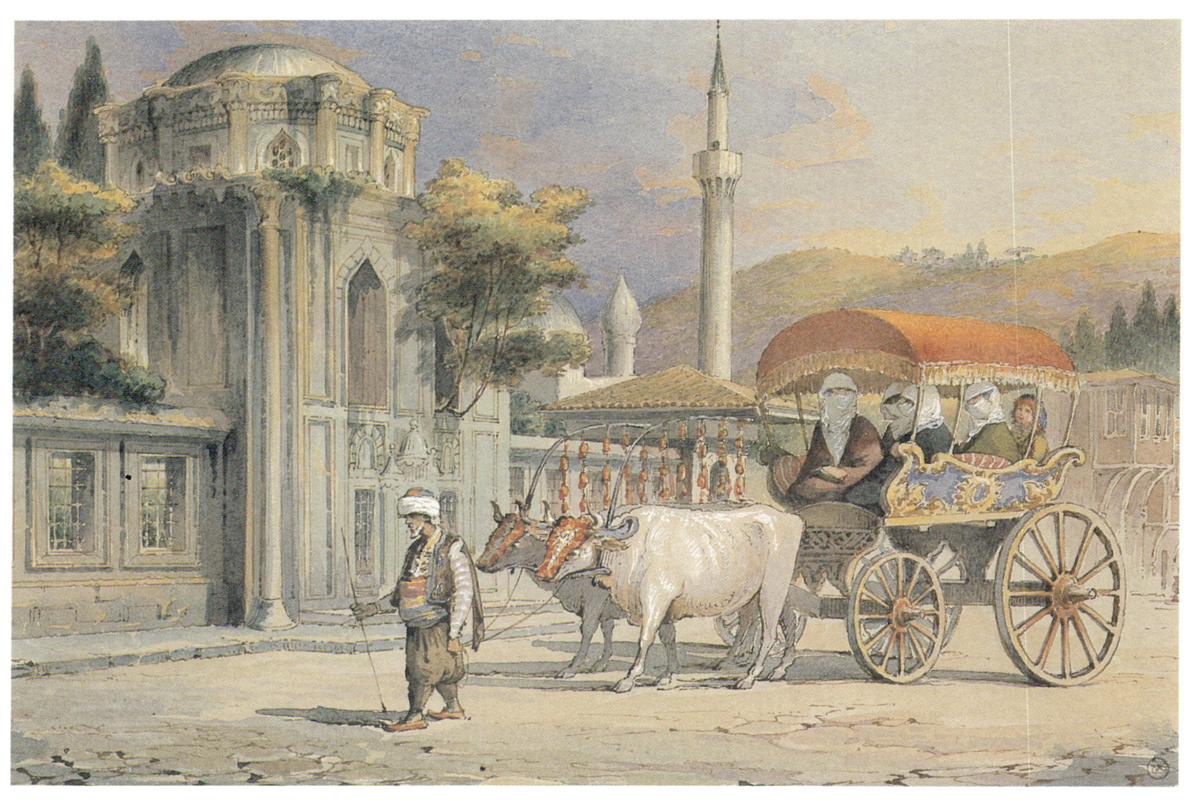

38 Ladies in an *Araba* c. 1843-50

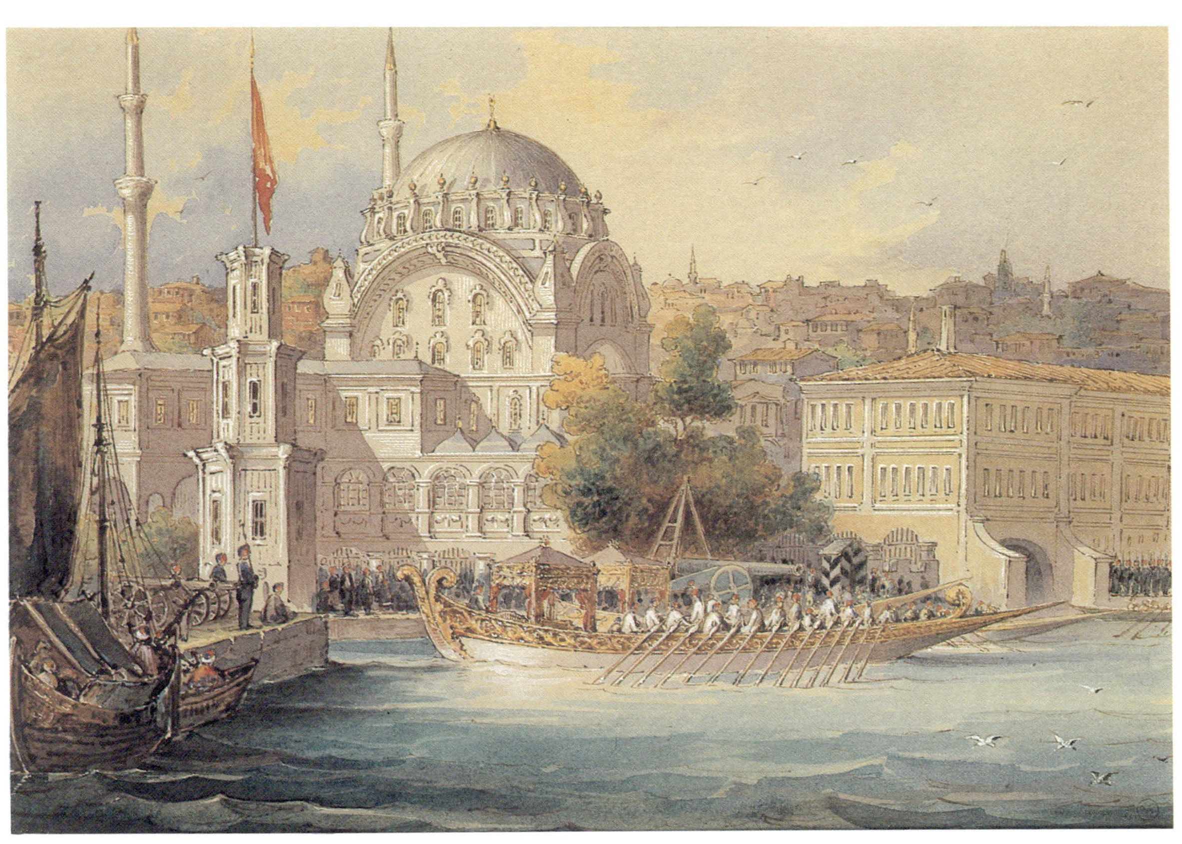

39 View of the Sultan's Barges in front of the Nusretiye Camii c. 1843-50

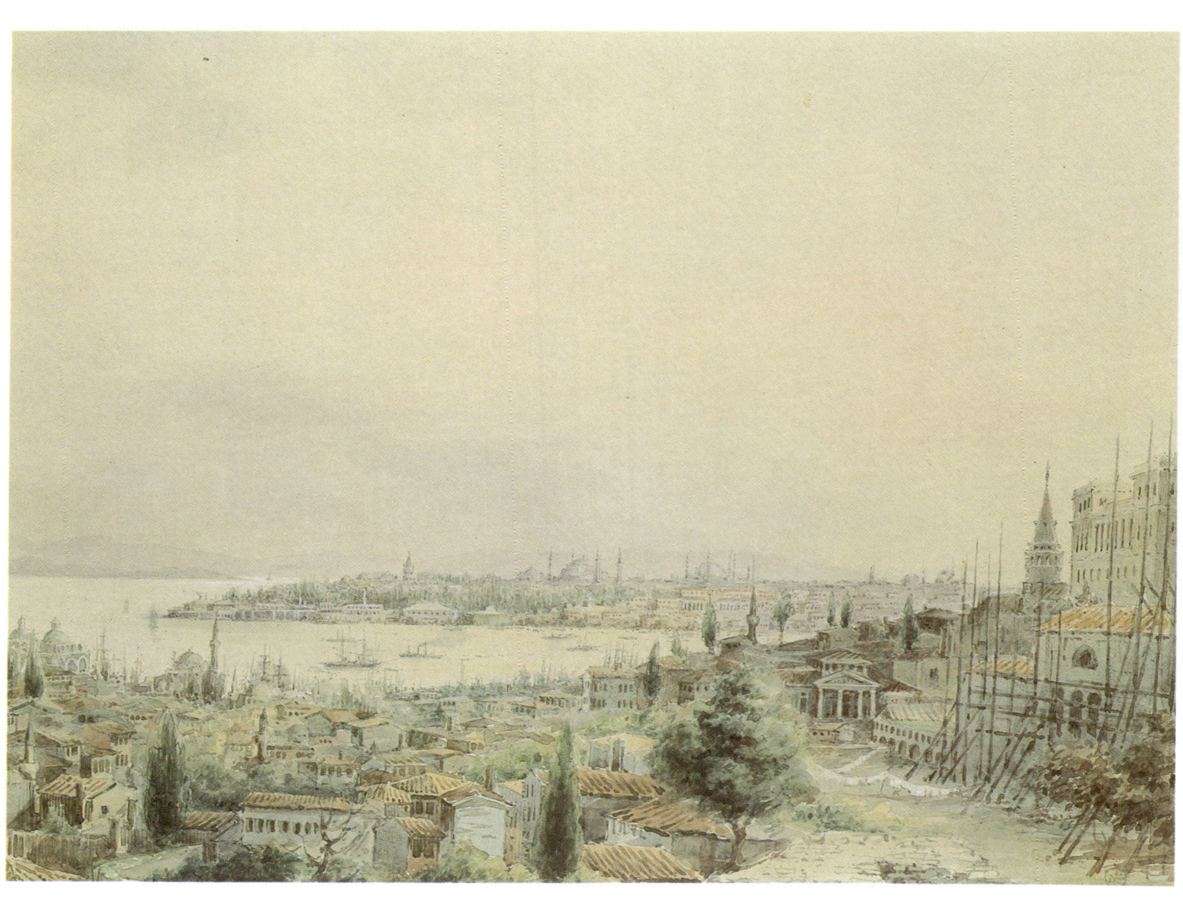

40 View of Constantinople from Pera c. 1843-56

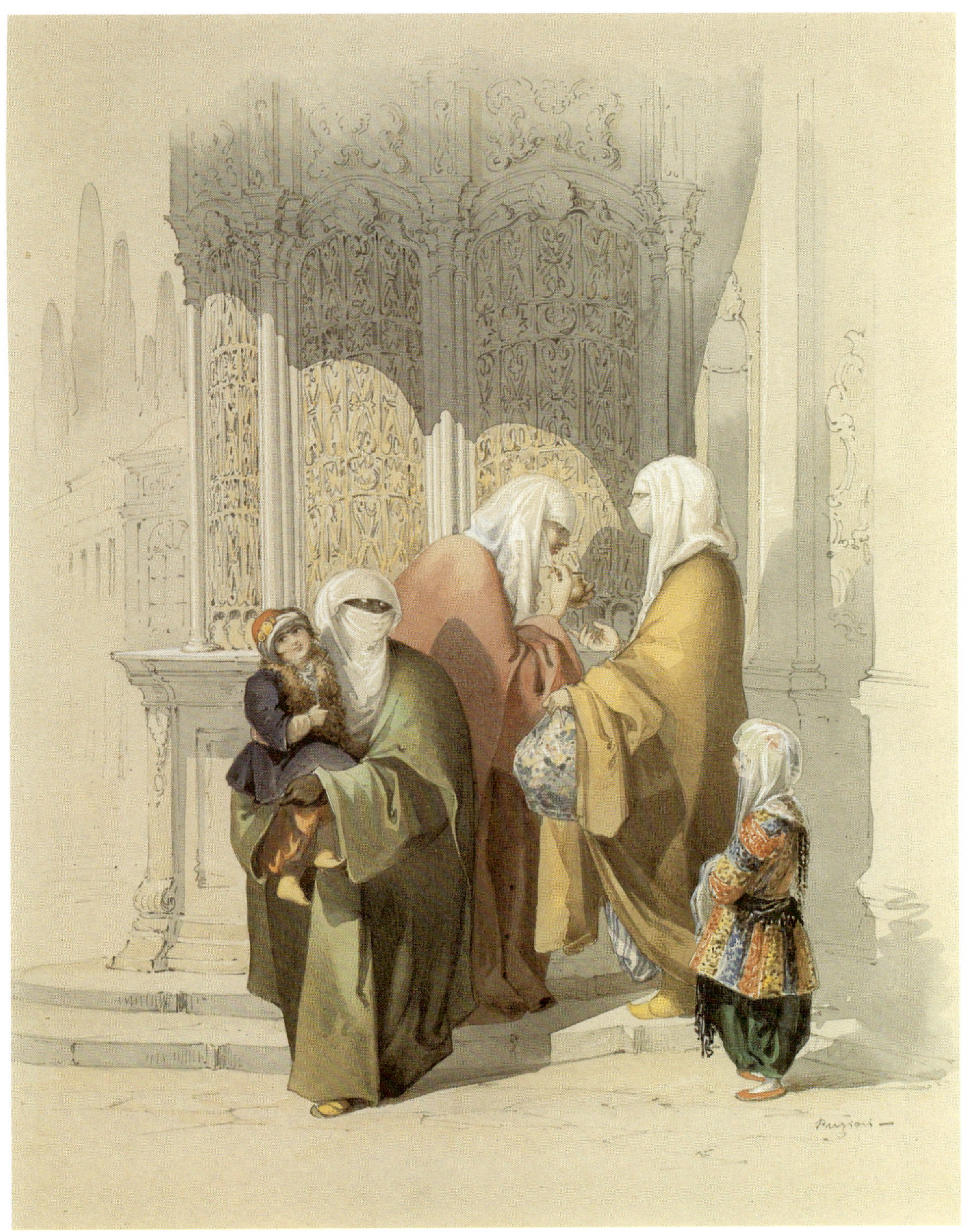

42 Women at a *Sebil* or Street-Fountain c. 1845

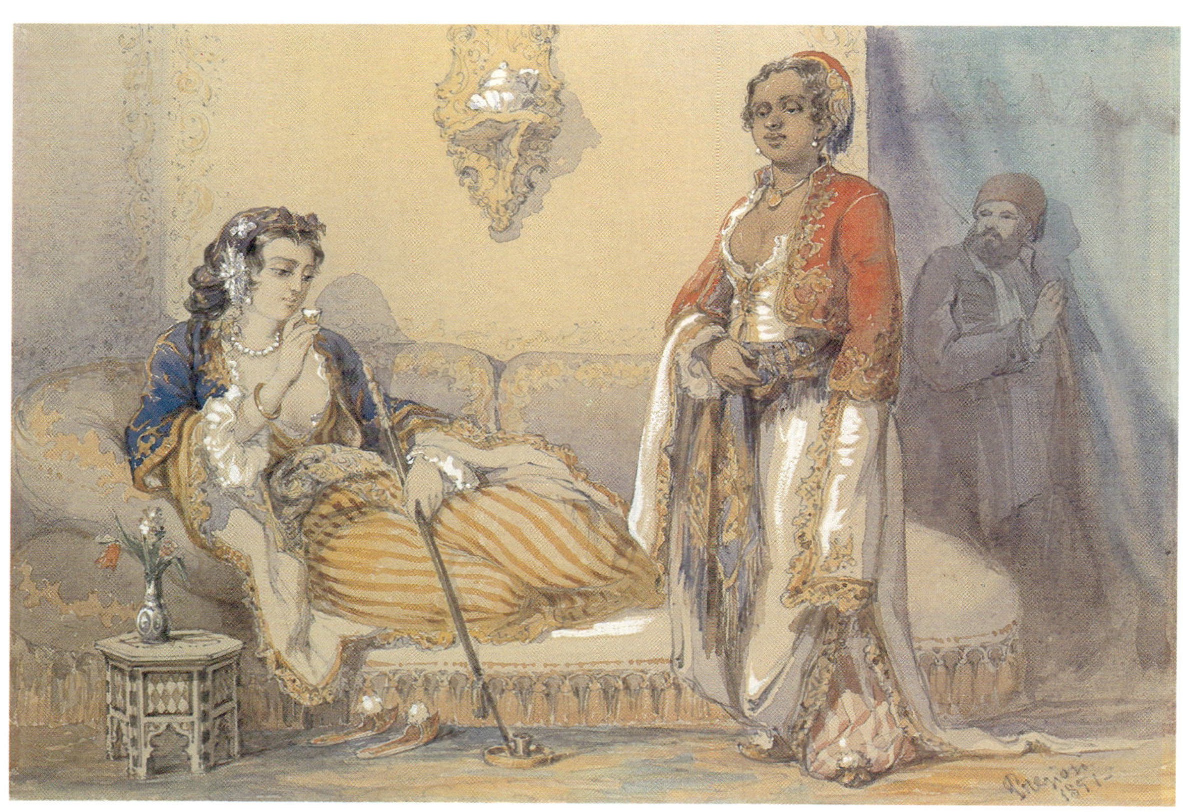

43 Interior of a Harem 1851

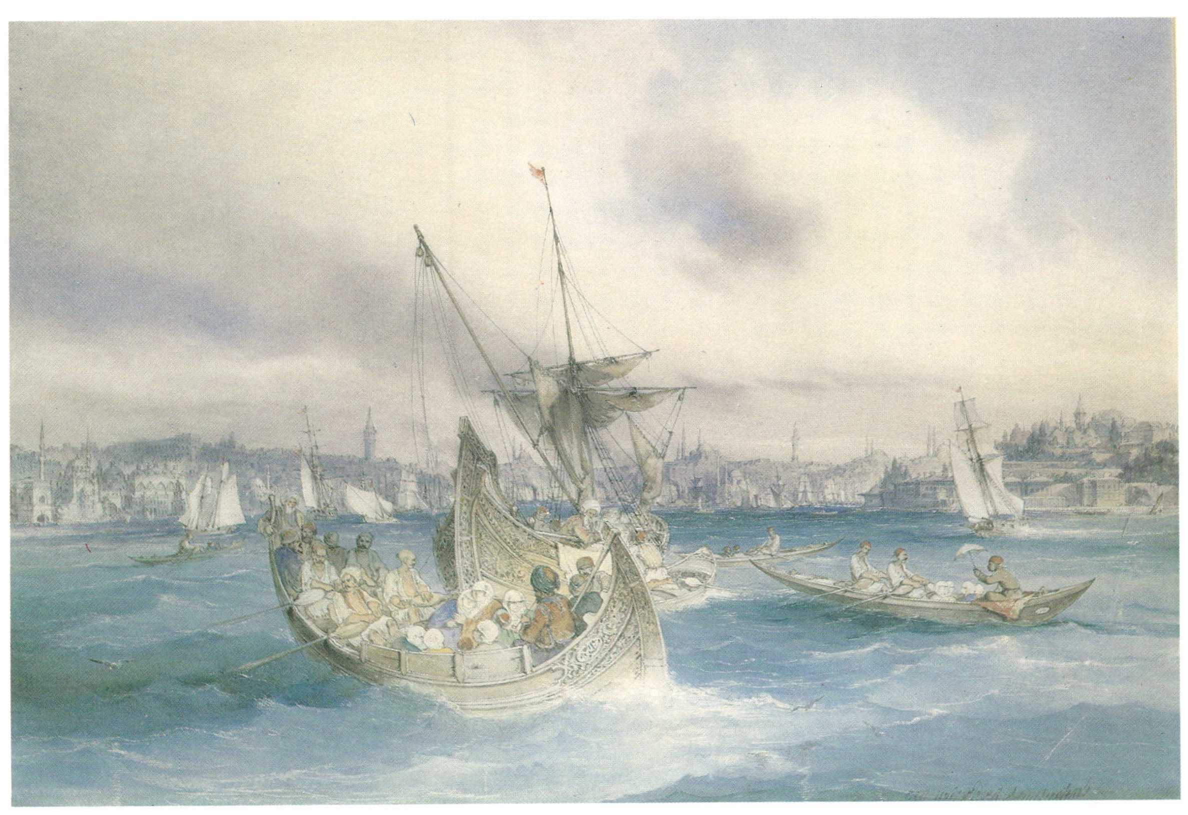

45 The Entrance to the Golden Horn 1852

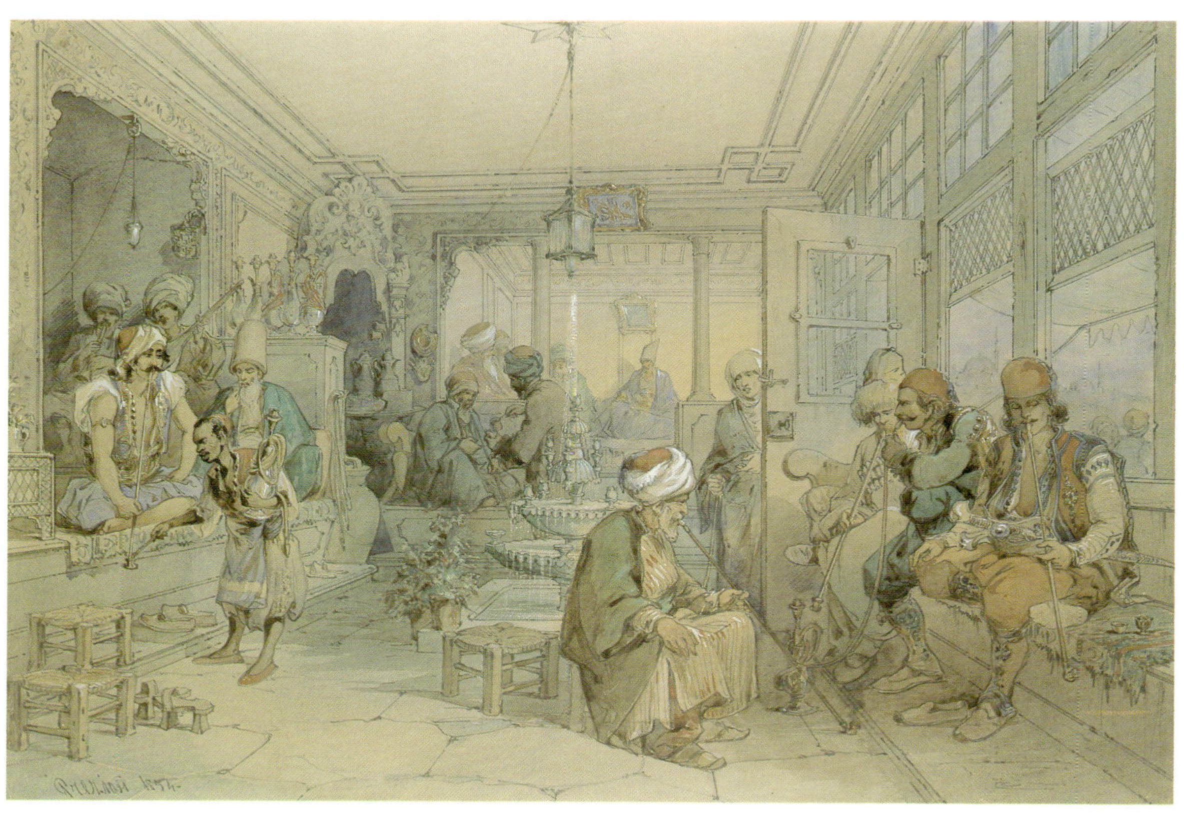

46 A Turkish Coffee-House, Constantinople 1854

Catalogue note

Preziosi transcribed Turkish and other foreign words phonetically into Italian. English-speaking travellers rarely agreed on English forms of Turkish words and spelling was very variable until language reform and the introduction of latin script in 1928. To avoid confusion the Turkish words in the text have been given in their modern spelling according to the dictionary *Redhouse Yeni Türkçe-Ingilizce Sözlük, Istanbul*, 1979. This rule has not been rigidly applied where an English form has established spelling and usage; for example we use *odalisque* not *odalık*.

Furthermore, some of the readings of Preziosi's inscriptions on his pictures are conjectural, especially the names. These too have been given a modern transcription but some are quite uncertain and we would welcome any comments.

Dimensions are given in centimetres, height before width. The size given is the drawn area on the sheet.

The Catalogue

The following drawings are from a group of 30 bought on the art market in 1907. Three (not exhibited) are dated 1843, the probable date for the whole series, since the drawings are consistent with one another in style and composition. They are also similar, though of a higher quality, to a series in an album commissioned from Preziosi by Robert Curzon (1810-73; later 14th Baron de la Zouche) in 1844. This is now in the British Museum (Department of Prints and Drawings, 197 b 15). The subject of each drawing (pen and ink and watercolour, touched with white; approx. 26 × 18.2cm.) is identified with manuscript notes. Several are versions of those in the group shown here.

Those in the Victoria and Albert Museum series not exhibited are: *Two Jewish Women in an Interior*; *A Greek Boatman*; *A Syrian in the Suite of an Emir*; *Women and a Child*; *A Jewish Merchant*; *A Turk of the Middle Class*; *A Soldier*; *A Persian*; *A Circassian*; *A Kavas*; *Madame Guido, Lady Canning's Genoese maid*; *A Healthy Turk Smoking a Nargile*; *An Albanian*; *A Priest*; *A Turkish Woman*; *Ladies in an Araba*; *A Greek Woman*.

♦

1
An Armenian Merchant c.1843
Signed *Preziosi*
Pencil and watercolour touched with white
25.4 × 17.4
Victoria and Albert Museum (D.14-1907)

According to the inscription on the variant in the Curzon album this represents an Armenian, who were often silversmiths and jewellers by trade. This man is evidentally a *kaşıkçı* or dealer in spoons, judging by the contents of the glass cases beside him. Spoons had almost ritual significance in Turkey and they were often very elaborately and expensively worked in precious metals. The most extreme examples are the gem-encrusted and impractical objects which belonged to the Sultan, now on show in the Museum at Topkapı Sarayı.

2
Portrait of a woman c.1843
Signed *Preziosi*
Pencil, watercolour and metallic pigment, touched with white
23.5 × 20.4
Victoria and Albert Museum (D.16-1907)

The costume of wealthy women in Constantinople was extremely elaborate and expensive, often made up from figured silks and lavishly embroidered in gold and silver thread. The lengthy sleeves worn by this woman illustrate a fashion which may be a relic of the ancient belief among the Turks that it was improper not to cover the hands. Over her wide *şalvar* or trousers she wears an *entari* or dress divided at the skirt to give a shawl-like effect. The outfit is completed by a silk shawl wound around the waist. The decoration of the interior is a curious mixture of the Gothic (the window), the contemporary French style (the European fringing on the sofa), and Turkish (the inlaid mother-of-pearl table). This may be a portrait of one of the relatives of Preziosi's Greek wife, but there is no positive evidence.

3
A Greek Woman c. 1843
Signed *Preziosi*
Pencil, water- and bodycolour 18.6 × 18
Victoria and Albert Museum (D.17-1907)

The Greek women of Constantinople were renowned for their beauty. They could walk in Pera, the European quarter, unveiled, but sometimes they would venture out dressed in the Turkish style, wearing a veil and enveloped in a large outer garment called a *ferace*. This outfit enabled them to go about unmolested and, of course, anonymous, which occasionally favoured intrigues. By Preziosi's time, the costume of the Greeks has become very orientalised, a process which had started long before the Ottoman conquest. The Byzantine Empire had been influenced in its dress by eastern nations like Syria, particularly in the use of elaborate woven silks.

4
The Slave Market c. 1843
Signed *Preziosi*
Pencil and watercolour 19.5 × 17.5
Victoria and Albert Museum (D.18-1907)

The Esir Han or slave market was situated near the mosque of the Nurosmaniye. It was a series of wooden booths with galleries round a courtyard which was destroyed in one of the disastrous fires at the end of the 19th century and now almost no trace remains. The girl for sale here is a Nubian, sitting on a mat in the courtyard. The more expensive Circassian slaves were kept indoors and were only shown to prospective buyers. In Fisher's *Constantinople* (1839) the Rev. Robert Walsh described the scene with some perplexity, since a visitor would expect to see 'helpless victims overwhelmed with grief . . .' In fact, he said, 'He sees no such thing: they are singularly cheerful and gay, use every means to attract his attention, and in their various dialects, invite him to purchase them'. He and other commentators gloomily concluded that the promise of a life of luxury and ease overcame any scruples and natural distaste for being the concubine of a rich man. Walsh alleges that some Circassian and Georgian families deliberately encouraged their daughters to enter that life. However, he said that the Greek girls were an exception and 'appear dejected amid the levity that surrounds them'.

5
A Kurdish Warrior from the Region of Lake Van c. 1843
Signed *Preziosi*
Pencil, water- and bodycolour touched with white 23.8 × 18.3
Victoria and Albert Museum (D.20-1907)

On the version of this drawing in the Curzon album is the uncharitable inscription: 'Koord, from the neighbourhood of Lake Van. These are a race of thieves and murderers, they are a pastoral race; but make a foray at least once every year, when they burn and destroy, what they cannot take away. His trousers are of woolen [sic] stuff, his spear has a tuft of ostrich feathers at the top'. This description and perhaps Preziosi's drawing reflects popular prejudice. A later and much more sympathetic representation is the portrait of *Abdullah from Bitlis*, who, incidentally is wearing the same sort of distinctive turban as the warrior here (cat. no. 16). The simple tents like the one shown are still much used in Turkey in the summer.

6
A Persian in a Coffee-House c. 1843
Signed *Preziosi*
Pencil and watercolour touched with white 22.3 × 16.4
Victoria and Albert Museum (D.22-1907)

The distinctive pointed fur hat identifies this man as a Persian, as he sits in a *kahvehane* or coffee-house with a *nargile* or water-pipe. Customers used to bring their own tobacco and amber mouthpiece but the shop provided the rest of the equipment for smoking, including a piece of glowing charcoal for the tobacco bowl.

7
A Mevlevî in a Cemetery c. 1843
Signed *Preziosi*
Pencil and watercolour touched with white
19.4 × 17.8
Victoria and Albert Museum (D.25-1907)

The Mevlevî or Whirling Dervishes were usually depicted in the midst of their ceremonies in their *tekke* or convent. Preziosi here shows one meditating with his prayer beads in a burial ground. Traditionally the headstones of the graves were carved with a representation of the turban or headgear of the deceased. For women floral forms were carved instead. In the background can be seen several headstones of Mevlavîs with stone copies of the tall felt hat or *külâh* similar to the one worn by the subject of the picture. There is a variant in the Curzon album.

8
A Dervish with a Leopard-Skin c. 1843
Signed *Preziosi*
Pencil and watercolour touched with white
20.5 × 16.5
Victoria and Albert Museum (D.26-1907)

Itinerant dervishes were a common sight in Preziosi's Constantinople, many of them having made the long journey from Central Asia. They excited feelings of fascination and horror in European visitors because of their savage appearance, armed as they often were with axes and other weapons. Most were hostile to the Franks, regarding them as infidels who corrupted Muslims. This holy man has a leopard skin which he used as a *post*, a kind of carpet on which he would sit to meditate or preside over religious ceremonies in his order of dervishes. On a stick is his bowl for alms, made of a coconut shell. There is a variant in the Curzon album.

9
A Greek Priest c. 1843
Pencil and watercolour 24.2 × 17.4
Victoria and Albert Museum (D.32-1907)

Greek refugees were encouraged to return to Constantinople after the conquest by the Turks in 1453. The Sultan, Fatih Mehmet II (the Conqueror) permitted the Greeks to practice their religion under their Patriarch and encouraged them to trade and bring wealth back to the city which had been severely impoverished since the sack and occupation by the Latins from 1204. The priest exhibited here is shown in his house with ikons of the Virgin and St. Michael or St. George (a saint of Asia Minor) on the wall. Preziosi had married a Greek woman and had his studio in Pera, and thus had many contacts in the Greek community.

10
A Barber c. 1843
Pencil and watercolour 22.6 × 17.9
Victoria and Albert Museum (D.33-1907)

Many of the coffee-houses or *kahvehanes* doubled as barber shops. Some races preferred to have shaven heads beneath their turbans or headgear, and, judging by the kind of hat beside him, the Armenian in this picture is taking advantage of this service. A mirror on a stand and other items of equipment are clearly visible on the shelf. An inhabitant of Constantinople could go to his favourite place of resort, take coffee, talk with his friends, smoke, be shaved and listen to a story or music, all for a trifling sum.

11
A Duck-Seller c. 1843
Pencil and watercolour 19.2 × 17.3
Victoria and Albert Museum (D.38-1907)

There were thousands of different pedlars in the streets of Constantinople and Preziosi here depicts a man selling what the Turks call *yeşilbaş* (literally 'green-head'), equivalent to the North European mallard drake but a somewhat larger and more colourful variety, considered a delicacy.

12
A Bulgarian Shepherd c.1843
Pencil and watercolour 16.2 × 17.8
Victoria and Albert Museum (D.39-1907)

In order to keep the capital city supplied with meat, large flocks of fat-tailed sheep were fattened and driven to Constantinople by their shepherds of various races. According to the Curzon album, in which there is a variant, this particular shepherd is a Bulgarian. Dogs were not used to drive the sheep, who knew and followed their shepherd, but were employed to keep off wolves and thieves. They were (and are) exceptionally fierce. The Bulgarians still export lamb but now to Iran via Turkey in huge container lorries.

13
A Simit-Seller or Simitçi c.1843
Ink and watercolour 23.5 × 19.6
Victoria and Albert Museum (D.41-1907)

There are still many *simit* sellers in Turkey, complete with the traditional portable tripod stand (*sehpa*) and tray (*tabla*). However, the picturesque costume is no longer worn. A *simit* is a kind of bread roll shaped into a ring and covered in sesame seeds, best eaten fresh as they become tough quite quickly as they cool. The *simitçi* is shown peddling his wares to a Greek girl and boy accompanied by their negro servant.

14
A Tatar c.1843
Pencil and watercolour with touches of white 20.4 × 15.8
Victoria and Albert Museum (D.43-1907)

This man in splendid uniform is, according to an inscription on a version in the Curzon album, a 'Turkish Tatar, or government courier. They ride night and day sometimes for 40 days, without stopping'. The '40 days' may be an exaggeration as it is a common expression in Turkish simply meaning 'a long time'. The couriers were originally recruited from the race of Tatars, those magnificent horsemen of Turkic stock, fierce descendents of the Scythian hordes whose name is now mis-spelt in English as Tartar. There are still a large number of Tatars in the Soviet Union.

♦

The following group of portraits is from a series of 31, acquired on the art market by the Victoria and Albert Museum in 1900. They were once assembled in an album, but whether by Preziosi himself, or a member of his family, or subsequently, is not known. Those not exhibited are:– *An Indian Dervish*; *Daut, a Serbian*; *A Muslim from Mecca*; *A Woman from Renkköy on the Dardenelles*; *Abdul Gazi from Egypt*; *Mattia, a Croatian*; *Agbut from Daghistan*; *Papa Demetrios from Mount Athos*; *A Muslim from the Crimea*.

15
Ibrahim, an inhabitant of Khokand, aged 35
Inscribed *Ibraym-Abitante del Kokan dell' età di 35* Dated *19 Maggio 1852*
Pencil, water- and bodycolour touched with white 25 × 19.1
Victoria and Albert Museum (D.16-1900)

Khokand was formerly the main city of a khanate in Turkestan situated in the western ranges of the Tien-Shan mountains. It was annexed in the 19th century by the Russians in their inexorable drive for colonisation eastwards and became part of the province of Ferghana. It is probable that Ibrahim would have spoken a form of Turkish which would have been intelligible in Constantinople (and to Preziosi) despite the great distance between the two places.

16
Abdullah, a Kurd from the region of Bitlis
Inscribed *Abdullah Curdo delle vicinanze di Bitlis* Dated *25 Maggio 1852*
Pencil and watercolour 33 × 25.6
Victoria and Albert Museum (D.17-1900)

The Kurds are an ancient people speaking an Indo-European language, whose lands are now divided between Turkey, Iran and Iraq.

Bitlis is an attractive town near the western edge of Lake Van in Turkey but once was a centre for the infamous Kurdish brigands similar to those described by J.J. Morier in *Hajji Baba of Isphahan*, 1824. Abdullah is wearing a splendid high turban typical of his race.

17
Elias, a Jacobite Priest from Mardin
Inscribed *Elias. Prete Jacobi da Mardin. Mesopotamia* Dated *26 Maggio 1852*
Pencil and watercolour 28.1 × 22.5
Victoria and Albert Museum (D.18-1900)

The Jacobite Christians are followers of the monk Jacobus Baradaeus who, in the 7th century preached the Monophysite doctrine of the one incarnate nature of Christ. This subtle theological error earned them the implacable hatred of the Catholics. A small number of these heretics still live near Mardin in Eastern Turkey, not far from the Syrian border, saved from annihilation by their isolation and their toleration by Muslims. The sect is described in Edward Gibbon's *Decline and Fall of the Roman Empire*, 1776-88, chapter XLVII.

18
An Indian Dervish from Lucknow
Inscribed *Dervisce Indiano di Luckno*
Dated *10 giugno 1852*
Pencil, water- and bodycolour touched with white 27.5 × 21.5
Victoria and Albert Museum (D.20-1900)

The Islamic world has no monastic tradition but certain of its holy men have always embraced poverty in order to intensify their vision of God. Some travelled great distances and lived by requesting alms which it was the duty of the devout to give. There were many different kinds of dervishes (literally those who have renounced the world) and they were often credited with extraordinary powers, such as healing and magic. The artist has not indicated what brought this dervish all the way from Lucknow, the historic capital of the province of Oudh in northern India.

19
An Indian from Calcutta
Inscribed *Indiano da Calcutta*
Dated *11 giugno 1852*
Pencil and watercolour touched with white
32.1 × 23.5
Victoria and Albert Museum (D.21-1900)

In Preziosi's time about a third of the population of Calcutta, capital of Bengal in north-east India, were Muslims. Many of them were merchants and the turbaned man shown here may have been a dealer in Indian shawls or some other textile. The Turkish idiom *Hint kumaşı* (literally *Indian cloth*) describing any object which is expensive and rare, (sometimes ironically,) derives from the ancient tradition of trade with India.

20
Constantino Sisopulos, a Greek from the district of Lokris
Inscribed *Costatino* [sic] *Greco da Dimos Loridos* Dated *12 Giugno 1852*
Pencil and watercolour touched with white
27.5 × 24.6
Victoria and Albert Museum (D.22-1900)

This fierce warrior has a massive sword or *yatagan*, with its distinctive handle, stuck into his belt, along with a pistol. On his chest is an impressive array of silver jewellery, no doubt containing prophylactic charms to protect him in battle, although their original purpose was as a series of belts for a powder horn and bullets.

21
A Dervish from Bokhara
Inscribed *Dervisce di Bohara*
Dated *15 Giugno 1852*
Pencil and watercolour touched with white
25.6 × 21.4
Victoria and Albert Museum (D.23-1900)

The city of Bokhara in Turkestan was the centre of religious life in Central Asia. In Preziosi's time it had a large number of mosques and it is said, 80 *medreses* or Islamic theological colleges for students. It was also a centre for the unofficial groups of holy men or dervishes like the one depicted here. This dervish also wears a leopard skin (see cat. no. 8).

22
Mustapha, a Muslim from Batum
Inscribed *Mustafa Musulmano di Batum (Lasistan)* Dated *18 Giugno 1852*
Pencil and watercolour touched with white
24.5 × 18.6
Victoria and Albert Museum (D.24-1900)

Batum is a town on the south-east coast of the Black Sea, now just over the border from Turkey in the Soviet Union. The inhabitants of this section of coast were known as the Laz people (hence the name of the place, Lazistan). The Lazes, generally renowned for their strength rather than their intelligence, were popularly (and no doubt unfairly) the butt of various humorous stories in Turkey.

23
Hanna, a Greek from Antioch
Inscribed *Hanna Greco di Antiochia*
Dated *19 Giugno 1852*
Pencil and watercolour 24.5 × 20.5
Victoria and Albert Museum (D.25-1900)

Antioch, now Antakya in Turkey, is an ancient city mentioned in the Bible as the place where the disciples of Jesus were first called Christians (Acts II:26) and where the Gospel was preached to the Greeks as well as to the Jews. Hanna, with his splendid turban, may have been a descendent of that group of gentiles whose example was followed by so many.

24
Ali, a Muslim from Medina
Inscribed *Ali Musulmano -da Medina*
Dated *1 Decembre 1852*
Pencil, water- and bodycolour touched with white 24 × 20.7
Victoria and Albert Museum (D.26-1900)

Medina was the holiest city of the Islamic world after Mecca because it was there that the Prophet Muhammad took refuge after his Hegira or Flight from Mecca in 622 AD. He lived there until his death and was buried in a mausoleum in the El Haram Mosque. Sacred relics of the Prophet, including a hair from his beard, were also kept in Constantinople in the Imperial treasury and can still be seen in the Museum at Topkapı Sarayı.

25
Pavel Cholagov, a Georgian from Tblisi
Inscribed *Pauli Ciolaghoff Giorgiano da Tiflis*
Dated *4 Decembre 1852*
Pencil and watercolour 31 × 23.2
Victoria and Albert Museum (D.28-1900)

This Georgian is wearing the distinctive *kalpak* or black lambswool hat typical of the Türkmen areas. Tiflis, now Tblisi became the capital of Russian Caucasia after its occupation and annexation by the Russians in 1802. The inhabitants were famous for their metalwork, especially the engraved and inlaid decoration produced by the silversmiths and gunsmiths.

26
Isaac, a Karaite Jew from Hasköy near Constantinople
Inscribed *Isach Ebreo da Haschioy (Constantinopli)* Dated *5 Decembre 1852*
Pencil and watercolour 28.5 × 21
Victoria and Albert Museum (D.29-1900)

The Jews who lived in Hasköy were members of the schismatic Karaite sect who had broken away from the main body of orthodox Jewry as early as the 8th century AD. Some of them had settled in Constantinople in the 10th century, living near where the Yeni Cami now stands, until the whole quarter was destroyed by fire in 1660. They were resettled by the Sultan Mehmet IV at Hasköy (literally 'royal village') on the upper reaches of the Golden Horn. There are still about 50 families left in the village, now a suburb of the city.

27
Trehem [?] Walid 'Abdullah, an Arab from Iraq
Inscribed *Trehem Viled Gabdullah-Babilonia* Dated *1854*
Pencil and watercolour touched with white
28.2 × 23.7
Victoria and Albert Museum (D.32-1900)

Babylonia, now part of modern Iraq, was the name of the fertile area between the Tigris and the Euphrates which nurtured many ancient civilisations. The site of Babylon itself is about 60 miles south of Bagdad and the Arab depicted here is typical of the proud people that lived in that area. He is wearing the distinctive headgear and robes of the region.

28
Timo, a Christian from Bulgaria
Inscribed *Thimo Christiano dalla Bulgaria*
Dated *1854*
Pencil, water- and bodycolour touched with white 28 × 23.2
Victoria and Albert Museum

The Bulgarians had been under the domination of the Turks since 1393 and did not finally throw off the last vestiges of their rule until 1908 when, after a series of bloody guerilla wars and revolts, Bulgaria became an independent kingdom.

29
Âdile Hanım, a Turkish woman from Constantinople
Inscribed *Hadilé Hanum Turca di Constantinopoli* Dated *1854*
Pencil and watercolour 27 × 24.5
Victoria and Albert Museum (D.34-1900)

This sensitive study is one of a very few straightforward portraits by European artists of Turkish women, who at this time would not ordinarily unveil themselves in front of a Turkish male, let alone a Frankish infidel, unless he was related in the correct degree. It is not known how Preziosi managed to take this likeness but the friends he made among the Turks may have helped him. Âdile's face is the reality that visiting western Europeans tried to glimpse behind the veils women wore in the street. Her broad firm face and steady gaze belie the image of the simpering beauty that existed in the untutored imaginations of Orientalist painters who never visited the East.

30
Hacı Hadi, a Persian from Ispahan
Inscribed *Hagi Hadi Persiano da Esfahan*
Dated *1854*
Pencil, water- and bodycolour 30.8 × 22.5
Victoria and Albert Museum (D.35-1900)

A *hacı* is the term used for a Muslim who has fulfilled the exhortation of the Prophet Muhammad to go on pilgrimage to Mecca. There were a large number of Persian merchants in Constantinople in Preziosi's time, many of them staying at the 'Persian Han' or caravanserai where they would indulge in the Persian sport of ram fighting with specially bred heavy-weight rams. This man is wearing the tall lambswool hat typical of these merchants.

31
An Albanian from Jannina
Inscribed *Arnaut da Jannina* Dated *1854*
Pencil water- and bodycolour touched with white 29 × 23.5
Victoria and Albert Museum (D.36-1900)

Albania was a western province of European Turkey from 1478 and remained so until 1912. The Turkish name, variously written Arnavut, Arnaut and so on, often appears in travellers' accounts. Because of the frequency of feuds and vendettas, the Albanians had a reputation for being fierce and war-like and in the 19th century they were alleged to be the best soldiers in the Turkish army. Ali Pasha, a Muslim Albanian of Tepellen, led a revolt against the Turks and made his headquarters at Jannina which was and is a wildly romantic site on the edge of a lake. He almost gained independence from the Turks in 1821-23 but they prevailed and he was defeated and executed. The melodramatic events of this cruel man's life has fascinated Europeans ever since. An account of Albania and Ali Pasha as seen by Lord Byron is given by his travelling companion, J.C. Hobhouse in *A Journey through Albania and other provinces of Turkey in Europe and Asia to Constantinople*, 1813. The Albanian depicted here looks relatively placid but they were normally shown as swaggering bullies with knives, sword and pistols thrust into their belts, carrying muskets, the very epitome of primitive warriors.

32
Iuvan Verbizga [?] from Montenegro
Inscribed *Iuvan Verbizga [?] Montenegro*
Dated *1854*
Pencil and watercolour touched with white
33.6 × 18.5
Victoria and Albert Museum (D.39-1900)

According to a 19th century *Gazeteer* the Montenegrins were 'a race of primitive mountaineers . . . a brave, warlike, and simple people, noted for their honesty and chastity. They live in small stone houses, in small villages'. Their territory was a mountainous region in the Balkan peninsula between Herzogovina and Albania, which after many vicissitudes is now part of Yugoslavia. The Montenegrins had resisted the Turks who retained only partial control in the incessant guerilla war that lasted centuries. The name 'Montenegro' is an Italian translation of the Slavic words for 'Black Mountain'.

33
Musa, a Hoca from Kashgar
Inscribed *Musa-hogia da Casgar (China)*
Dated *1855*
Pencil and watercolour touched with white
22 × 22.3
Victoria and Albert Museum (D.40-1900)

A hoca was a teacher of the Qur'ān, the basis of a Muslim education. He is shown holding his *tespih* or string of prayer beads. He is also wearing a crochet linen *takke* or skullcap similar to ones still to be seen on the heads of devout Muslims today. Kashgar was the centre of Islamic learning in Eastern Turkestan, a famous place of pilgrimage. Musa may have come to Constantinople with one of the caravans bringing silks and porcelain as they had done for many centuries. There are still Turkic speaking Muslims in China and several mosques in Chinese cities have recently been restored.

34
Ibrahim, a Muslim from Sennar
Inscribed *Ibraim -Da Sunnar* Dated *1856*
Pencil and watercolour touched with white
27.5 × 25.2
Victoria and Albert Museum (D.43-1900)

Sennar is a city in the Sudan, 160 miles south-east of Khartoum, on the Blue Nile. It was one of the stages in the trade route from the interior of Africa up river to Cairo; it was also renowned for its oppressive heat. The ancient kingdom of Sennar was invaded by the forces of Muhammad Ali, Pasha of Egypt, led by his son Ismail, in 1821.

35
Hagiadur, an Armenian from Erzerum
Inscribed *Hagiadur Armino da Erzerum*
Dated *1856*
Pencil and watercolour 28.3 × 22.5
Victoria and Albert Museum (D.45-1900)

Erzerum is a strategic military town situated high in the mountains of Eastern Turkey, not far from the Kara Su or Black Stream, the source of the Euphrates river. It has been the scene of many tragedies in the series of wars with Russia in the 19th century and was occupied by them in the First World War. It once had a large Armenian population represented by the man depicted here.

36
A Bektaşi Dervish from Bosnia
Inscribed *Dervisce-Musulmano da Bosnia*
Dated *1856*
Pencil and watercolour touched with white
29.5 × 18.3
Victoria and Albert Museum (D.46-1900)

The dervishes of Bosnia (now part of Yugoslavia) were reputed to be particularly devoted followers of Hacı Bektaş, as were many people in Turkey itself. They have no real equivalent in the West but they were politely contemptuous of Muslim or any other orthodoxy, they ate and drank in Ramazan and were loosely described as free-thinkers. They appear to have considered that they had reached such a pitch of spiritual development that the constraints of harsh dogma no longer applied to them. Books of humorous stories, about Bektaşis happily confounding the bigots, are still published in Turkey today. Naturally, the orthodox regarded them as drunken rogues and Preziosi perhaps reflects this opinion in his mischievous portrait of the old man.

♦

37
Ladies by a Fountain near the Sweet Waters of Asia
Signed *Preziosi* Inscribed *Asia*
Dated *20 October 1843*
Pencil, watercolour and metallic pigment
28.1 × 18.3
Guiterman Collection

The Sweet Waters of Asia was the name given by Franks to the meadow surrounding the Küçüksu (literally 'little stream') which flows into the Bosphorus on the Asian side north of Constantinople. Like its counterpart on the European side it was a favourite place of resort, though with fewer permanent structures. The fountain shown in this picture was built by the Valide Sultan (the Queen Mother) Mihrişah in 1796 and it stands very near the shore. The Turkish ladies are sitting for their picnic in traditional style on a carpet, looking a little nervously at the painter. As only the eyes were visible above the veil, immense amounts of meaning had to be conveyed by a glance and there were even special ways of walking which the perceptive Turk would understand.

38
Ladies in an *Araba* c.1843-50
Brown ink and watercolour with touches of white 17.7 × 25.5
Victoria and Albert Museum (D.46-1907)

One of the chief pastimes of Turkish women who spent much of their time in the seclusion of their houses was a trip in an *araba* or carriage, drawn by splendidly caparisoned oxen or horses. They would go to visit friends or to picnic at numerous places around Constantinople, usually a meadow with running water, such as the Sweet Waters of Asia or of Europe. The Sultan's Harem would also visit these picnic places, suitably veiled and guarded, as well as the royal palaces and their gardens on the Bosphorus. The all-purpose word *araba* still means in Turkish a cart or carriage but nowadays is usually the word for motor-car or even motor coach.

39
View of the Sultan's Barges in front of the Nusretiye Camii 1843-50
Pencil, water- and bodycolour 18.7 × 25.4
Victoria and Albert Museum (D.45-1907)

The Nusretiye Camii was built between 1822 and 1826 by Sultan Mahmud II and was completed just after the extermination of the Janissaries; hence its name, which means 'victory mosque'. It is virtually next to the barracks at Tophane, which was the cannon foundry across the Golden Horn from the old city. The influence of baroque is obvious on the mosque's Armenian architect Kirkor Balyan who had studied in Paris. The elaborate gilded *kayıks* or boats belonging to the Sultan always elicited excitement and interest from his subjects and from foreigners who wanted to catch a glimpse of the mysterious despot who spent most of his life in the seclusion of his palace.

40
View of Constantinople from Pera c.1843-56
Pencil and watercolour touched with white
20.8 × 26.4
Victoria and Albert Museum (D.44-1907)

Frequent earthquakes have taken their toll in Constantinople but the city suffered most from disastrous fires which ravaged the wooden buildings, tinder-dry in the hot summers. The tall cylindrical fire-tower (still there) of Galata which was reconstructed by the Ottomans for watchmen of the municipal guard is just visible to the right of the picture. In the background, across the Golden Horn can be seen the buildings of the palace complex of Topkapı Sarayı, built on the end of the promontary called Saray Burnu (Seraglio Point). The magnificence of the palace was in the extent of its relatively small but beautiful buildings set in wonderful gardens with views towards the other six hills of the city, the Golden Horn and the further shore of the Bosphorus on the Asian side. When Topkapı Sarayı was abandoned by Sultan Abdülmecid I in the 19th century he moved to a new palace at Dolmabahçe along the Bosphorus which was a massive western European style building with imposing façades.

On the shoreline to the left can be seen the mosques Kılıç Ali Paşa Camii and the Nusretiye Camii, still well-known landmarks.

41
The Sweet Waters of Europe c.1845
Signed *Preziosi*
Pencil and watercolour 24.5 × 31.8
Eyre and Hobhouse Limited

The Sweet Waters of Europe was the name given by Franks to the area at the confluence of two streams, the Alibey Suyu and the Kağıthane Suyu, which form the source of the Golden Horn. On the banks and on the surrounding meadows many pavilions and palaces were built by sultans and their courtiers and it became a favoured place for the outings and picnics of the people of Constantinople. On the left of this picture is a splendid *köşk* (a kind of summer-house or pavilion) in a baroque style, hung with awnings, almost certainly belonging to the Sultan. On the right is a strange entwined serpent column which is a reduced and restored copy of the famous one from Delphi, in the At Meydanı or Hippodrome in the city. There had been at least two attempts to use the waters of the stream for a paper-mill (*kağıthane*) but both were financial failures. Sadly, the whole area (unlike the Sweet Waters of Asia) has now become an industrial wasteland.

42
Women at a *Sebil* or Street-Fountain c.1845
Signed *Preziosi*
Pencil and watercolour touched with white
29 × 22
Searight Collection

There were many *sebils*, some of them very elaborate, in the streets of Constantinople, since they were its main source of water. They were often built as an act of piety by rich people for the public, water provision being regarded as a particularly meritorious act in the warm climate. The Turkish women here have paused to drink, one of them having lowered her veil in order to do so, while the negro servant holds the small boy. His fur-edged coat indicates that his father was a man of substance. While the little girl is dressed in a vividly coloured outfit, the women are completely encased in their *feraces* or cloaks. The similarity of figure style and subject-matter to *Women and a Child* in the Victoria and Albert Museum's series of Constantinople characters (not exhibited; D.23-1907) suggests a similar date around the mid 1840s.

43
Interior of a Harem
Signed *Preziosi* Dated *1851*
Pencil and watercolour touched with white
18 × 26.3
Searight Collection

Preziosi probably used models to recreate this harem scene which as an infidel Frank he would not normally be allowed to witness. However, there is nothing in this decorous interior which is impossible or unlikely and it may be based on a visit to the house of one of his Turkish friends. The furniture and fittings show western European influence, particularly in the curious rococo wall bracket and the fringed sofa in place of the traditional raised wooden platform covered with carpets. By the middle of the 19th century French style in interior design was fashionable in Turkey, especially a degenerate form of the rococo. The woman smoking a *çubuk* or pipe has probably filled it with a mild and aromatic tobacco mixture favoured by harem inhabitants. In her right hand she holds a coffee-cup while the negro slave, possibly a Nubian, stands awaiting a command. In the background the Turkish master of the house is entering the room. A version of this composition, dated 1852 and allegedly painted for the Empress Eugènie, is much less restrained, its details deliberately pandering to the popular western idea of a harem, based on *Arabian Nights* imagery (see Lynne Thornton et Jean Soustiel, *Mahmal et Attatichs. Peintres et voyageurs en Turquie, en Egypte et en Afrique du Nord*, Paris, 1975, cat. no. 12, illustrated p.23).

44
The Sandal Bedesteni or Silk Market, Constantinople
Signed *Preziosi* Dated *1852*
Pencil and watercolour 36.1 × 52.8
Guiterman Collection

This large 16th century structure is part of the enormous complex of covered market buildings in the centre of the city. Market scenes were a favourite theme of Preziosi's, perhaps because he could include exotic types from many places, who had come to buy and sell in one of the greatest centres of trade in the world. The sketch is rapid but includes a vast amount of detail. To the left is a neo-classical structure for the market officials, guarded by a soldier; then a group of dervishes; in the centre a sweet-meat seller; on the right a seller of shawls and a female customer. The Sandal Bedesteni, recently restored, is now used for carpet auctions but not, alas, normally crowded with exotic folk jostling and bargaining for the silks of Bursa and India.

45
The Entrance to the Golden Horn
Inscribed *Constantinople by Preziosi*
Dated *1853*
Pencil and watercolour 51 × 72.5
Searight Collection

The entrance to the Golden Horn was one of the finest natural harbours in the world. In the background is Seraglio Point (Saray Burnu) with gardens and pavilions spreading up the hillside, and the skyline of the old city. In the right background are Pera and Galata with the Galata fire-tower on the skyline and, on the shores of the Bosphorus, the buildings of Tophane. In the foreground are examples of the type of craft then plying the waters of the Bosphorus: on the left a light caïque (*kayık*) of the kind used to ferry passengers from the Asiatic to the European shores; the heavy barge in the centre was used to transport people to and from the villages along the shores of the Bosphorus; at anchor is a typical trading galley. The oarsmen or *kayıkçılar* row with the strange local form of oar with bulbous handles. Because the small *kayıks* were very frail, passengers had to exercise great care getting in and out and had to sit still, especially if the weather was rough, since they were easily overturned.

46
A Turkish Coffee-House, Constantinople
Signed *Preziosi* Dated *1854*
Pencil and watercolour touched with white
40.7 × 58.8
Searight Collection

This is a fine example of Preziosi's close observation of contemporary life; the sketch, though rapid, is filled with a mass of detail. A large gallery of characters is depicted, all of them evidence of the cosmopolitan character of Constantinople. On the left can be seen a *saz* or group of musicians, a Greek with a *çubuk* or long cherry-wood pipe, a negro lad applying a glowing piece of charcoal to the bowl, carrying at the same time a *nargile* or water-pipe, and a Mevlavî or whirling dervish in his distinctive felt hat or *külâh*. In the background are merchants, including a Persian. In the foreground is another merchant with a *çubuk* and at the door an unveiled beggar-woman on her rounds. To their right are a Circassian with cartridges on the front of his coat, and two more Greeks smoking. The coffee-house itself is a luxurious 19th-century baroque structure, probably on the shore of the Golden Horn. Equipment is clearly shown: on the left is row of *nargiles* with some spare tubes and a large water-pot; behind them, in the corner, the stove for heating the coffee and the charcoal for the pipes. Next to the Greek in the right foreground are a coffee-cup (*fincan*) and its metal holder (*zarf*). In the centre is an elaborate fountain which cooled the room in summer. Travellers were extremely impressed by coffee-houses such as this and the first one in London in 1652 was modelled on a Turkish example.

47
View of the Bosphorus with the Allied Fleets at Anchor
Signed *Preziosi* Dated *1854*
Pen and ink, pencil and watercolour
25 × 35.5
Searight Collection

During the Crimean War the British, French and Turkish fleets anchored in the bay of Büyükdere in the Bosphorus north of the city, within sight of the entrance to the Black Sea. The war generated an immense amount of interest in Turkey and its inhabitants and such views of 'the seat of war in the east' were very popular with the British; a similar but much larger example is dated October 1853 (Government Art Collection no. 1807).

48
The Sweet Waters of Europe c.1855
Signed *Preziosi* Inscribed on the back *Sweet Waters of Europe Bosphorus*
Pencil and watercolour touched with white
26.5 × 35.5
Searight Collection

The Turks have always loved the open air, presumably inheriting this characteristic from their nomadic tent-dwelling ancestors in Central Asia. Boats were a relatively recent experience but they readily took to them for pleasure trips. This scene shows the head of the Golden Horn where boats could be hired to take passengers as far as the Bosphorus. The large trees are probably plane-trees whose broad leaves provided shade from the hot sun. They are often found planted in centres of ancient towns or in the precincts of mosques, and are still popular in Turkey today.

49
The Turkish Letter-Writer or *Arzuhalci*
Signed *Preziosi* Dated *1855*
Watercolour, bodycolour and chalk
35.1 × 29.8
The National Gallery of Scotland

This is a preliminary composition sketch for one of the lithographs [plate 23] in *Stamboul. Recollections of Eastern Life*, 1858 (see p.00). Its exaggeration of features and the evident speed with which it has been drawn calls to mind the caricatures of Daumier, but in the lithograph these aspects have been toned down. Preziosi also altered the man's gaze to stare meditatively at his client instead of, as here, looking at his work, and replaced the fat woman with one more attractive. The *arzuhalci* was very necessary as few people were literate; he also wrote out petitions to Government officials and tax-collectors.

50
A View across the Bosphorus c.1855-60
Pencil and watercolour touched with white
18.5 × 34.3
Searight Collection

This view is taken from the European side of the Bosphorus, looking over the roofs of Pera towards the Asian shore, the Kız Kulesi (the Maiden's or Leander's Tower) visible in the left background on its tiny island. The white buildings are the barracks at Scutari (modern Üsküdar). A steamship, probably British, is shown in midstream, sailing towards the Sea of Marmora on the right.

51
The Cemetery of the Crimean Heroès
Signed *Preziosi* Dated *1856*
Pencil and watercolour 29.5 × 44.5
Searight Collection

This cemetery was the last resting place of the British soldiers who died in the nearby Selimiye Barracks during the Crimean War; several of Florence Nightingale's nurses are also buried here. Across the water is the European shore with the city of Constantinople on its seven hills and the entrance to the Golden Horn. Aya Sofya, the Tower of the Vezirs and Seraglio Point are clearly visible. The picture once belonged to Thomas F. Hughes, Oriental Secretary at the British Embassy, 1859-75.

52
A Water-Carrier or *Saka* and a Woman at a *Sebil* c.1857
Pen and ink, wash and watercolour
35.9 × 28.2
The Al-Mashreq Gallery

This is the finished drawing from which the lithograph (plate 13) in *Stamboul. Recollections of Eastern Life*, 1858 (see p.10). The old *saka* with his leather water-skin is waiting to fill his container before going to sell water for a trifling sum to the thirsty people in his district. He is taking the opportunity to leer at the pretty woman adjusting her veil.

53
A Gipsy Encampment outside Bucharest
Signed *Preziosi Bucharest* Dated *'69*
Pencil and watercolour 35.2 × 53.5
Searight Collection

Preziosi visited Bucharest, the capital of the two then recently united Rumanian principalities, in 1868 and 1869. The large number of drawings made by him on these two trips range from atmospheric wash studies of river and sky to highly detailed figure compositions illustrating the folk-life of Rumania. The majority are still in Rumania, in the Muzeul de artà al Republich Socialiste România. This lively drawing, though rapidly executed, packs in much visual information. It incorporates some of the same elements as one of the series of large finished watercolours (of which there are at least 41), *View of Bucharest from Filaret*, dated *1 juillet 1868*. Both focus on the gipsies and their distinctive cart with its curious axle and springing arrangement, and both include in the foreground the buxom girl carrying an unusually turned and carved wooden water-pot. Both also contrast the picturesque squalor of the encampment with the neat buildings of wood and stone in the background, but in the larger version, the skyline of Bucharest is at a much greater distance, with a consequent increase in the sense of space. The entire group shows that Preziosi's powers of observation did not decline as he grew older (see Busuioceanu, and Golfin, *op. cit.*).

54
Stamboul Recollections of Eastern Life
Imp. Lemercier, Paris 1858
Victoria and Albert Museum

For details of this publication, see *Introduction* and *Preziosi's Publications*.

Preziosi's Publications

Stamboul Recollections of Eastern Life, Imp. Lemercier, Paris, 1858: contains a frontispiece, incorporating the title, and 29 colour lithographs titled in English and French: *Druggist's Shop*, *Mendicant Dervishes*, *Vendors-Arnauts*, *Gypsies*, *Turkish Ladies Walking*, *Guard House*, *Jews*, *Silk Bazaar*, *Turkish Carriage*, *Keepers' Croats*, *Sweetmeat Shop*, *Boatmen*, *Water Carriers*, *Pilaff*, *Greeks*, *Cup of Coffee*, *Sultan Bajazet's Courtyard*, *Araba*, Caiques on the Bosphorus (untitled), *Burial Ground*, *Turning Dervishes*, *Eunuch of the Seraglio*, *Public Letter Writer*, *Albanians*, *Coffee House*, *Sweet Waters*, *Porter*, *Loaf Vendors*, *Interior of a Coffee House*. Most prints are signed *Preziosi* and dated 1857 or 1858.

These details refer to the copy in the Searight Collection, as do the plate numbers given in cat. nos. 49 and 52; copies may also be found in the National Art Library, London, the Bibliothèque Nationale, Paris, and Topkapı Saray, Istanbul.

Stamboul Souvenir d'Orient, Imp. Lemercier, Paris, 1861.
This appears to be a reprinted edition of the 1858 volume, with a different title page by Jules Mea. There is a copy in the Victoria and Albert Museum, Department of Prints and Drawings.

Souvenir du Caire, Imp. Lemercier, Paris (?1863): contains 20 colour lithographs. There is a copy in the British Library.

Stamboul Moeurs et Costumes: contains 28 colour lithographs (price, 200 francs).
Le Caire Moeurs et Costumes: contains 20 colour lithographs (price, 150 francs).
Both these are reissues of the earlier volumes, by Canson Libraire-Editeur, Paris, 1883, as part of an *Encyclopèdie des Arts Decoratifs de l'Orient*, with introductions by Victor Champier. Each plate is numbered, and lettered *Preziosi del et lith*. Copies may be found in the British Library.

Views in Rumania
According to Öndeş (*op.cit.*, p.XV), Preziosi's watercolours made in Rumania in 1868 and 1869, were reproduced as lithographs in Bucharest in 1873. However, the compilers of this exhibition have been unable to trace the volume.

Select Bibliography

Julia Pardoe, *The Beauties of the Bosphorus. Illustrated in a Series of Views of Constantinople and its Environs, from original drawings by W H Bartlett*, 4 parts, London, 1837-39.

Reverend Robert Walsh, *Constantinople and the Scenery of the Seven Churches of Asia Minor*, 2 volumes, London, 1839.

Théophile Gautier, *Constantinople of To-Day*, (translated from the French by Robert Howe Gould), London, 1854.

Adolphe Thalasso, *L'art ottoman Les peintres en Turquie*, Paris, 1911.

Chambers's Concise Gazetter of the World, ed. David Patrick, assisted by William Geddie, London, 1914 edition.

Al. Busuioceanu, *Preziosi*, in a series *Collection Apollo. Artistes Etrangers en Roumanie*, Bucharest, 1935.

Bernard Lewis, *The Emergence of Modern Turkey*, London, 1961.

Raphaela Lewis, *Everyday Life in Ottoman Turkey*, London, 1971.

Osman Öndeş, *Istanbul aşığı ressam Preziosi*, Istanbul, 1972.

Osman Öndeş, 'Un peintre amoureux d'Istanbul: Amadeo Preziosi', in *Türkiye Turing ve Otomobil Kurumu Belleteni (Revue du touring & Automobile Club de Turquie)*, Istanbul, Janvier-March 1974, pp.21-23.

Gülseren Ramazanoğlu, 'A Maltese Painter in love with Istanbul Amadeo Preziosi', in *Hilton International Istanbul Magazine*, Volume 6, No. 23, Fall 1975, pp.8-9.

Marin Nicolau-Golfin, *Preziosi*, Bucharest, 1976.

Sarah Searight, *The British in the Middle East*, revised edition, London, 1979.

Paul Mizzi, 'Amadeo Preziosi' in *Heritage. An Encyclopedia of Maltese culture and civilisation*, No.42, April 1982, pp.827-34.

John Freely, *Blue Guide Istanbul*, Tonbridge, 1983.

List of Lenders

Al-Mashreq Gallery, Eyre and Hobhouse Limited, Guiterman Collection, National Gallery of Scotland, Searight Collection.